Anger
RECONCILIATION

Anger
RECONCILIATION

A new approach
to conflict that brings
people together
instead of driving
them apart

JAMES OFFUTT

SEL PUBLICATIONS
Syracuse, New York

Library of Congress Card Number: Txu1-333-590

ISBN 9780615225845

Published by:
Sel Publications
Syracuse, NY

This book is dedicated to my loving wife Connie who started me on the journey to learn about my emotions and to Syracuse Teen Challenge students and director, Dave Pilch, who launched me on the quest to express anger in a godly way.

Acknowledgements

I wish to thank my Lord and Savior Jesus Christ for His direction, not only for helping me establish and teach my "Anger Reconciliation" class at Teen Challenge, but also for leading me to write this book. I strongly believe that the Holy Spirit inspired me throughout the project. Also, I am very grateful to my devoted wife, Connie, who helped me with ideas and prayed continuously for the book; Dave Pilch for starting me with this topic; the students at Syracuse and Orlando Teen Challenge for their encouragement to write a book; Tim Bennett, my editor, for corrections and helpful ideas; my friend Emmanuel Awauh for his corrections; my friend Rick Hemmes for his ideas; Terry Hobin of Teen Challenge for his positive testimony on RAA; and both Daphne Mayer and Ruth Cameron of Man in the Mirror Ministry for their valuable input.

Contents

Introduction

This book is a direct result of the class on "Dealing with Your Anger" that I started in 1993. Dave Pilch, the Director of Syracuse Teen Challenge, handed me *The Anger Workbook* and asked me to teach the class for the Teen Challenge students. I had never taught or read about anger at all, but I took up the challenge and started the class. At Syracuse Teen Challenge we found over 15 years that 90% of the men came with problems with their anger. Promise Keepers found anger problems to be the third most important issue for men. Anger, however, can also be a problem for women, which I discovered when I conducted my seminar in various churches.

My source material, besides *The Anger Workbook*, was mainly the Bible. I initially called the class "Anger Management." Upon further reading and prayer to God, however, I sensed God wanted me to study the Scriptures in reference to anger and to change the class name to "Anger Resolution." During this time I started getting more material from the Bible, *The Soul Care Bible*, the Internet, *The Anger Workbook, The Anger Trap, Anger Is a Choice, The Dance of Anger, Coping with Your Anger, Making Peace with Conflict, Design for Wholeness, Boundaries* and *Man to Man*. God continued to work on me in my Bible reading making me more aware of the importance of achieving reconciliation with our anger. Therefore, I felt compelled to change the name of the class again to "Anger Reconciliation." Additionally, this led me to the biblical principles that formed the basis for Respectful Assertive Anger (RAA).

Over the years, I also have been reviewing my own anger expression, which I have changed gradually from "stuffing" anger to more assertiveness. God helped me to develop RAA 13 years ago. As I began using it successfully in my own life, I taught it at Teen Challenge centers in Syracuse, New York and Orlando, Florida as well as in local church settings, which has proved life changing to literally hundreds of people.

Most of the testimonies in this book come from students in these classes: the others are from friends or people I knew. The names in all the testimonies have been changed except my family and Terry Hobin who gave me permission to use his name when he gave such a positive endorsement of RAA. He graduated from the first phase of four months at Syracuse Teen Challenge and then went to the second phase of eight months at Rehresburg, PA. His endorsement came after he had expressed many doubts about the usefulness of RAA in his life. He is one of the many people who have changed their anger expression from negative anger to RAA with good success. It is my hope that this book will open people's minds and hearts to change from negative anger to positive anger and receive those same results.

The biblical principles of respectful assertiveness help create the opportunity for true anger resolution and reconciliation for everyone. Many people have seen for the first time how anger can be used positively in their lives. We can now confidently resolve our angry situations without hurting others or constructing walls in our relationships by actively seeking harmony (reconciliation) with others. I also hope that this book will encourage more pastors to talk to their parishioners about dealing with their anger in a Christian way.

— *Jim Offutt*

Chapter 1
Anger is?

My 16-year-old son, Andrew, entered the house shouting angry words as he came into the den where I stood. He then walked over to the kitchen door. As I started to talk to him, he swung his fist hard at the door—bang! He smashed through the solid core door still hollering with his face contorted with anger. There he stood with his arm through the door screaming foul language. This was the face of violent anger—rage.

My natural reaction would have been to shout him down. However, 12 months earlier, I had taught students at Syracuse Teen Challenge about how to handle their anger as Christians, and I knew I had to act differently. God had shown me through prayer and Bible study some biblical principles and I saw this as a golden opportunity to put them into practice. Praise God! These principles resolved the situation and Andrew never hit anyone or anything in the house again. He is now 31. These principles form the basis of this book. I am hopeful they will help other Christians to learn how to express their anger in a Christian way. Little did I realize that teaching the anger course at Teen Challenge was the start of a new spiritual walk for me. I'm amazed at how much I have learned on the subject over the past 15 years of teaching.

Anger is not an easy emotion for anyone to handle. Generally, for most of us, we express it in one of two ways—either we are afraid of it and we run from it by holding it in, or we lose control and express it explosively. Using either of these polar opposite reactions, however, always produced negative results for me. In fact, they only fed my desire to avoid anger whenever possible. Many Christians are taught at early ages that anger is bad and even considered a sin. A biblical instruction on anger can be found in James 1:19-20: *". . . Everyone should be quick to listen, slow to speak and slow to become angry, for man's anger does not bring about the righteous life that God desires"* (NIV- Note all quotes from the Bible are from the NIV except where noted). This Christian attitude against anger is also stated in *Coping with Your Anger* by Andrew Lestor: "In the early centuries of church history, men and women training for religious vocations were taught not to pray when they were angry. This idea continues into the present and particularly affects us if we are handling anger poorly." Frequently, Christian leaders use the word anger to imply negative results. They send a subtle message that anger in ANY form is bad.

Holding anger in is too often the recommended Christian approach by parents or Christian leaders. Proverbs 20:3 confirms this approach: *"It is to a man's honor to avoid strife, but every fool is quick to quarrel."* To express anger can create messy situations that result in broken relationships. We are taught that we are "nice" Christians when we hold our anger in. This concept is what I believed for a vast majority of my life. The irony is, by doing this, I also held in the whole range of emotions such as joy, happiness, sadness, laughter, love, etc. that make us real people. I basically had a fear to express anger because of the negative results I had seen with my father's aggressive anger. The anger that I held in, however, still eventually came out in negative ways such as in passive-aggressive behavior, or depression. We will examine these negative approaches to anger in Chapter 2. We shall then find out what God wants us to do with our anger. He wants us to have a freedom to express our anger, but in a life giving way as discussed in Chapter 3.

Anger is defined by *Webster's New Third International Dictionary as* "a strong feeling of displeasure . . ." (Note: all future definitions will come from this dictionary unless another reference is specifically noted). Anger is an intense emotion that can result in hostility or new understanding. The end result all depends upon what path we choose to follow. Anger develops when we find that rejection and judgment are the norm rather than love and understanding. When this happened to me, I felt a climate of pessimism.

Anger also energizes the body to fight against physical and/or emotional threats to our lives. The book *Design for Wholeness* by Brother Loughlan Sofield ST, Sister Juliano Carrell SHCJ and Sister Rosine Hammett CSC explains: "anger is a form of energy . . . I (each person) determine how the energy created by anger will be changed and released."

Anger is also a secondary emotion that occurs after we feel a threat from fear or frustration. God created anger as a way to deal with threats to us. I like the anger equation that Andrew Lester used in his book, *Coping With Your Anger.* The equation is a succinct approach to visualizing the anger process:

$$\text{"threat} \rightarrow \text{anxiety} \rightarrow \text{anger."}$$

We perceive a threat, real or imagined, from a fear or frustration, which causes us to feel anxiety. The anxiety leads to anger being expressed.

There are events or triggers that often occur in our lives, which can set off an emotional response leading to anger. These anger triggers follow:

THREATS

Disrespect. This trigger comes from a feeling of being put down or not respected. We all seek some outside approval so when disrespect happens, it can injure our feeling of self-worth. Such emotional injuries are especially strong when we did not receive unconditional love as a child. Disrespect can take many forms: when someone uses verbal putdowns, not listening, or ignoring us. These actions can cause us to feel insignificant and less valued as a person resulting in great anger. The amount of anger will often times depend upon the person's emotional strength. In Esther 1:17, Queen Vashti shows disrespect to the king: "*. . . King Xerxes commanded Queen Vashti to be brought before him, but she would not come.*" The nobles then complained that their wives who would hear of such behavior would disrespect them as well.

In this instance, the wrath of the king and the nobles led the king to remove the queen from her position.

> Don, a leader at Teen Challenge, sat with tears running down his cheeks as he described how he had been humiliated. Others were consistently putting down his abilities and calling him names. At first, he believed them to some extent. Finally, the disrespect made him angry and he was determined to stop his tormentors. Don knew God's Word tells us to respect all people. Remembering this, he confronted his tormentors and told them to stop. This action turned around the situation for his betterment and he was smiling and thanking God as he spoke to me.

Violated physically. Anger occurs when someone hurts us either physically, or with sexual abuse once, or over a period of time. We feel under the physical control of someone else.

Such a situation leads to an atmosphere of fear in a person, which dominates his or her life. This leads to a strong desire to escape this torture and take revenge on the perpetrator.

> Joe, a student at Orlando Teen Challenge, spoke about how his uncle had sexually abused him from an early age. He felt trapped as the abuse went on month after month. He was also filled with such hatred that he wanted to kill his uncle, but he knew he was too small. "Oh, if I were only bigger," he thought. Then, he could exact his revenge. This hatred controlled his life and as he grew up he sought relief through drugs. The drugs did medicate his pain but they also led to his addiction, which eventually brought him to Teen Challenge and my class on anger. At one point during the class he

became so overwhelmed with his pain he cried out that he wanted to leave immediately and get drugs. With the help of another student who had experienced the same abuse but had overcome it, we both talked to Joe about how to find freedom from his pain. The other student had been successful in getting released from the anguish by constantly giving it to God. We used this experience to show Joe how to find freedom from his hurt. Joe did seem to calm down and the class prayed for him. Overtime, Joe overcame his pain with the Holy Spirit's help.

Violating our values. Everyone has values, whether Christian or not. We develop them through a wide variety of ways including our families, our peers, our education, the media, or our personal experiences. As Christians, we are asked to stand for such biblical principles as: worshipping God, loving our neighbor, serving others, being faithful in our marriages, defending human life, and equal rights, etc. One example of standing up for godly values is in Daniel 3:18 where Shadrach, Meshach and Abed-Nego told King Nebuchadnezzar: "*. . . let it be known to you, O king, that we do not serve your gods, nor will we worship the gold image which you set up.* "

Often worldly values are completely opposite to those of the Bible including: materialism, power, abortion, racism, adultery, letting the end justify the means, lying, cheating, etc. We can be controlled by the worldly values of our friends or authority figures (parents) in our lives. Christ asks us to stand up for His values and He will protect us. Conflicting values can represent one of the major areas where even believing Christians get into angry situations. *The Anger Workbook* by Frank Minirith and Les Carter point out how values relate to anger ". . . we sometimes feel angry when we realize others are insensitive to our most fundamental convictions."

When I was working in the International Division of

a bank in NYC, I had a new boss take over. He was
young, very energetic and lustful. Although married,
he would always pick up a woman at one of our
business receptions. He wanted me to do the same,
but I refused saying I was happily married. I still felt
his pressure to conform to his ungodly demands. He
kept tempting me until he finally punished me by
denying me my annual raise. Just before Christmas
he took me out for a talk when he fired me because
I was not a "team player." I was deeply hurt about los-
ing the job that had been a 14-year dream for me.
However, I knew that it was a test of my Christian
principles. God somehow protected me by moving
me to another department where the boss was a
good Christian. This change influenced my life for
good forever. Later, after I had moved to Syracuse, I
was blessed to be born again. I prospered while my
old boss and all his subordinates were later fired.

Essential needs. These are those needs that we must have to live a con-
tented life. These "needs" exclude our "wants" which include selfish
desires. God knows our true needs and wants to supply them, Phil.
4:19 says: *"And my God will meet all your needs according to his glorious
riches in Christ Jesus."* Thus, we have the confidence that God wants to
supply our needs. Unfortunately, our anxiety to get these needs met
plus our sinfulness can get in the way and prevent God from meeting
our needs. We also oftentimes feel that our wants are really needs, which
confuses us. These needs vary from person to person, but they usually include the following: respect (separated out because of its importance), relationships with others, safety, feeling valued by others, alone
time and the basic human needs (food, clothing and shelter). We get
angry when we perceive that others are denying us these powerful needs.
In *The Anger Workbook* by Frank Minirith and Les Carter, the authors
describe it this way: "The angry person demonstrates a weariness of

having to live without his or her basic needs being noticed by others."

FRUSTRATION

Frustration is defined as: "to be checked, balked or defeated in an endeavor or purpose." Frustration comes from other people or particular circumstances, which prevent us from meeting real or perceived needs. These frustrations usually occur repeatedly until we become aware what's really happening. Then we feel angry. Many frustrations are really minor irritations as Gary Oliver explains in his article in *The Soul Care Bible:* "Things that frustrate people the most usually have one characteristic in common—they really aren't very important."

Unfortunately, we have no control over when and how these anger triggers will occur. We all receive them throughout our lives. How we deal with them is our own choice based on our internal Christian values and training for expressing anger. Certain triggers elicit a more intense response because of our wounds and become our weak points for anger.

> Bill, a student at Teen Challenge, was not afraid to face explosive anger from other people. He seemed to handle these situations with ease. Yet, he would crumble quickly into intense anger when disrespected by another person. Bill's anger response reflected the wounds (weak spot) he received while growing up. He continued to have difficulty with this area during his stay at Teen Challenge.

We all have such anger triggers in our lives that make us vulnerable to anger. Our challenge is to discover these areas and deal with them in a godly way. This process shall be discussed in Chapter Four on how to reduce or eliminate these triggers from our lives.

What does the Bible say about anger as a Christian?

Colossians 3:8 says, *"But now you must rid yourselves of such things as these: anger, rage malice, slander and filthy language from your lips."* Note rage and malice are stages of ungodly anger.

Then again in Ephesians 4:31 we read: *"Get rid of all bitterness, rage and anger brawling and slander, along with every form of malice."* These verses ask us to get rid of anger. This leaves the implication that all anger, in any form, is not what God wants. Many in the Christian church have taught this mistaken idea of anger for years. The note for verses 4:28-32 in the *Life Application Bible* helps to clarify Paul's intent: "Paul warns us against . . . bitterness, improper use of anger . . ." This note qualifies that anger is wrong when it is expressed in an improper (ungodly) way.

Ephesians 4:26-27 clarifies the Christian approach to anger: *"In your anger do not sin. Do not let the sun go down while you are still angry, and do not give the devil a foothold."* In these passages, it is not anger in itself that is sinful; it is the failure to deal with anger in a godly way that is the problem. The note for verses 4:26, 27 in the *Life Application Bible* confirms this: "The Bible doesn't tell us that we shouldn't feel angry, but it points out that it is important to handle our anger properly. If vented thoughtlessly, anger can hurt others and destroy relationships." If anger is not expressed in a godly fashion, it is a sin. Also Satan can magnify the anger into rage or bitterness. Psalm 4:4 by David fortifies Ephesians 4:26 by restating: *"In your anger do not sin."* Thus, even the Old Testament says that anger is permissible. Finally, James 1:19 states: *". . . Everyone should be quick to listen, slow to speak and slow to become angry . . ."* All three Scriptures allow anger but caution how we express it.

This point is also explained in the *The Soul Care Bible* note for Ephesians 4:26-27. It states: "The Bible doesn't say, 'Never get angry.' It does say, however, 'Be angry, and do not sin.' Anger is a God-given, powerful emotion. Handled well, anger can cause positive change. Anger handled poorly, however, can cause great harm." Anger is a God-given emotion so anger, in itself, is not a sin.

Gary Oliver, in a section on anger in *The Soul Care Bible*, further amplifies the point about anger. "The Bible says *'Be angry and do not sin'* (Ephesians 4:26). This type of anger depends on the help and guidance of the Holy Spirit . . . As we learn creative ways to invest the God-given anger energy, as we approach anger from a biblical perspective, we can find one of the most powerful sources of personal motivation available." Consequently, anger is not only from God, but can be used for positive results.

Upon deeper review, the anger described in the first two passages represents anger that has not been resolved. Anger held in for a time becomes bitterness or wrath and this is not what God wants. He urges us to confront the other person in a godly way to resolve the anger. This method of dealing with anger, we call "positive anger" as discussed below. The challenge is that there usually is a valid reason for our anger. We just can't avoid anger as it can happen many times throughout the day. The problem is many of us lack the knowledge of how to "get rid" of it (or resolve it) without sinning. Most of the time we are prone to express it in a hurtful way to get revenge. I call this negative anger. Satan is looking to divide us as couples, families, churches and friends through our worldly approach to expressing our anger. Generally speaking, anger can be divided into two categories:

Negative anger is when I use my own will against God's plan for expressing my anger. I seek to get my own way (selfish anger) and violating (using or controlling) others for my own self-interest. Expressing anger in this way may seem best for me for a while allowing me to find temporary satisfaction. Success disappears with time because I am violating God's principle of loving my neighbor. Accordingly, I am sinning, which results in generating anger from others, which is what Satan wants. Most of us only express our anger in a negative way because we don't know any positive ways of expressing our anger.

Positive anger is when I use the Christian principle of loving to deal with and resolve anger for the benefit of both parties. This process is what Christ calls us to do with our anger. There are several types of positive angers, which are discussed in detail in Chapter Three. The goal of this book is to inform Christians about the value of positive anger, which involves anger reconciliation. Once Christians learn positive anger choices, I strongly believe they will choose only positive anger expression(s). This type of anger is a better choice because it produces a positive result for both parties in a conflict.

To clarify the differences, I list the following characteristics:

Characteristics	Positive Anger	Negative Anger
1. Spiritual	God controlling: use biblical principles to resolve.	God is not used: depends on self or worldly ideas.
2. Respect	Care is shown to the other party in voice and words.	Disrespect is prominent in speech and volume.
3. Listening	Tries hard to listen and understand the other person.	Usually does not hear or want to hear the other person.
4. Control	Tries to let God control. Seeks best for both parties.	Seeks self-control for own purposes.
5. Goal	Seeks resolving the issues to make the relationship better.	Seeks to win: doesn't care about the relationship.

These characteristics are explained in more detail in chapters two and three.

We learn our method of expressing anger from the following sources:

Our families. We are not born angry. God wants us to love each other. Love gets distorted in our families through legalism or abandonment. As we grow up, we see how anger is wrongly expressed or not expressed in the family. This daily modeling has a powerful effect on us as children. Thus, we often copy the way anger is articulated by our parents. Even if we hate the type of anger uttered, we will often tend to copy it. This intent is stated in Numbers 14:18 "*. . . Yet he does not leave the guilty unpunished; he punishes the children for the sin of the fathers to the third and forth generation.*" We see the lasting affect of negative anger modeling extending through the family for generations (generational anger).

> I remember my father shouting down my mother, my sister and me with his aggressive anger. He tried to control the situation with his explosiveness and intimidation. His expression of anger was so unappealing to me that I chose to go the opposite way and hold in my anger for years. My mother would just cry in response to my father's anger expression. My sister, at first, was intimidated and then let loose her aggressive anger. Our whole household was tense and on edge when dad was angry. This negative anger modeling influenced how my sister and I expressed our anger for years.

How did your family deal with their anger? How does that affect you and your anger today?

Personality. Each person's personality is distinct and develops over time. We may, by nature, be aggressive; thus aggressive anger feels more natural. Others may be more passive, or contemplative. Their anger may be more naturally held in, or expressed in passive-aggressive ways. As we mature, our personality may change, which could influence how we express our anger.

Experience. We may have originally used aggressive anger wrongly resulting in painful consequences like jail. This painful experience may cause us to change our way of expressing anger to the opposite direction—holding in our anger. We see the pain negative anger causes in us and others. In seeking to find other alternatives, we may copy the anger expression of a friend, or others we admire. This situation is especially true when the other person's anger expression seems to work. Over time these changes in expressing our negative anger yield the same negative results. These negative anger experiences may cause us to change our expression of anger several times over our lifetimes. Resolving our anger seems to be a painful illusion.

> Nora hated the heated angry outbursts from her father. She would go to bed sometimes shaking from the fear she felt from him. Being a more quiet and reserved person, aggressive anger did not feel comfortable to her personality. Her friend, Cathy, had a similar personality and they could empathize with each other easily. Nora realized that Cathy would get even with those who offended her with passive-aggressive anger. She would pretend to give in to someone, but do the opposite in a quiet way. This subtle anger pattern appealed to Nora, who adopted it for herself, but again, it brought painful results over time.

While we have little choice about our families, God calls us to begin to take responsibility for our anger as we experience life's trials. Gradually, we learn that our anger expression is really a selection of one of several choices. Seeking the godly choice takes prayer and God's direction. If anger is used negatively it can destroy relationships and cause us great pain. Finding positive expressions of anger builds relationships, brings new freedom and peace to one's life. Positive anger expressions will also give us greater self-confidence and stronger self-esteem in angry situations.

In summary, whether it is road rage, a movie *Anger Management,* or silence between church members, anger plays an increasing role in our daily lives. Consequently, it is becoming more important to understand what anger is and how to express it in a positive way as we have seen in the Scriptures.

Anger is a God-given emotion. It originates from a valid need to correct something that we perceive as a threat or frustration. Anger is really an early warning system that something has gone wrong. It is a secondary emotion that requires godly direction, or it can destroy our lives.

This book is designed to redefine the way we think about anger. In Christian circles, far too often, the word anger is discussed only negatively. This view is very disturbing and misses the value of positive anger. It is my desire to encourage the use of positive anger and discourage the use of negative anger in our lives. My goal for this book is to help everyone to start making positive anger the only choice for expressing anger.

Summary:

1. Anger is a feeling of displeasure: It is a secondary feeling caused by a threat or frustration.

2. Triggers that create anger include the following: threats to our security, disrespect, being violated physically, violating our values, failure to meet our essential needs and frustration.

3. Negative anger expression is using our own will against God's plan for expressing our anger.

4. Positive anger expression is using love to help us express our anger in a godly way.

5. Sources of anger are family, personality and experience.

Discussion Questions

1. Do you have any fear of expressing your anger? Why?

2. How do you express your anger? Has it been effective?

3. What kind of anger did you experience in your family?

4. How did you feel about that type of anger?

5. Do you see how positive anger could be used in your life?

Chapter 2
Negative Expressions of Anger: A Path to Pain

Negative forms of expressing anger represent those ways which anger is not resolved or reconciled to the benefit of both parties. God does not play a role in resolving negative anger expressions. As we discussed in Chapter One, anger arises when we perceive a threat or frustration to us. The anger formula is: **threat → anxiety → anger.** We get anxious about the threat, which causes us to get angry. Regrettably, we are so consumed by our need to correct the situation that we usually fail to respect the other person when expressing our anger. Frequently, we face a dilemma with our anger because we sense a hurt caused by the other person. Yet, we don't know how to express our anger in a loving way. This valid message may involve any, or all of the following: our own physical safety, important values, or our self-esteem.

Unfortunately, this important message gets lost in the sending because we express it in hurtful ways. Thus, the receiver of the message will, in most cases, not focus on the real message. He will instead feel the hurt caused by the words used and/or the delivery of the message. People using negative anger also have poor negotiating abilities to resolve angry situations. Consequently, the opportunity for dialogue is lost and mutual understanding is not possible.

We feel hurt or frustration, which creates anger towards the other person. By expressing our hurt in a negative way, we cause the recipient to feel disrespected and they usually retaliate with negative anger. As a result, we feel even greater pain. This cycle of negative anger countering negative anger may continue on for a while. No one knowingly wants to do this. We feel caught in a negative anger cycle because we don't know how to respond any differently.

The various types of negative expressions of anger are:

AGGRESSIVE ANGER

Aggressive anger is using a loud voice, swearing, shouting, hitting, pushing, etc. to express our anger. The goal of the person is to make sure he is heard. They may use physical force to enforce their message. In *The Anger Workbook* by Les Carter and Frank Minirth, people with aggressive anger have ". . . a focus that so strongly emphasizes personal needs there is a powerful insensitivity to the needs of others." Their own hurt dominates, which predisposes them to seek revenge. Therefore, they will use disrespectful language and emotion in their message. The receiving person will not want to hear or understand what is being said. The net result may often be that both parties become aggressive in their anger toward each other. Then, neither one ends up listening or trying to understand the other one.

The origin of aggressive anger starts in childhood. Children of aggressive angry adults see the model of their parents and/or classmates winning their arguments through loud voices and powerful actions. Seeing this success, they, in turn, will tend to replicate their parent's powerful anger expression. As adults, therefore, they expect others to listen and understand them when they employ those intimidation tactics. They soon discover, however, that this mode of expression creates the exact opposite of what they want—great resentment in the people around them. The Bible speaks against aggressive anger in Genesis 49:5-7 where Jacob is talking to his sons: " *'Simeon and Levi are brothers—their swords are weapons of violence . . . for they have killed men in their anger . . . Cursed be their anger, so fierce . . .'* "

The equation for showing aggressive anger, modifying the formula of John Lester in Chapter One, is the following:

**Aggressive anger modeling as a child → threat → anxiety →
aggressive anger → No resolution; pain continues;
others angry at us**

The negative modeling at childhood starts an aggressive pattern of anger that may continue in the person into his/her adult years. As a result, the person may feel that they are caught in an anger trap for life.

There is a strong need for control by the aggressive person. They seem like they are demanding: "You must listen to me and obey." This attitude usually reflects some inadequacies, or insecurities in the aggressor. This expression may work for a short time, but usually causes resentment to accumulate in the person receiving it. Eventually aggressive anger can damage or destroy relationships. There is no negotiating with such a person because of his single-mindedness and intense feelings. Consequently, personal freedom or differences of opinion are rejected. All these negative actions lead to negative results for everyone involved.

Some evidences of aggressive anger are:

Don't want to listen to others: constantly interrupting others when they are speaking. They are so intent in getting their viewpoint across that they don't listen and process what is said. This action makes dialogue and mutual understanding impossible. Accordingly, this attitude creates resentment in others who then become angry with them.

Seek to give others unwanted advice. People with aggressive anger tend to think their ideas are the only correct ones. As a result, they tend to be critical and corrective of others. Yet, they reject correction of their own actions or words. There is a noticeable lack of empathy, which creates distance with others. They have difficulty making deep friendships. In the book, *Coping with Your Anger,* Andrew Lester describes aggressive anger: "Some people are destructive with their anger because they have no cherished beliefs that prohibit them from openly attacking other persons when they are threatened. They simply don't care whether they hurt, ruin, or tear down with their anger." This shows aggressive anger's devastating force.

Emotionally they act like children: use pouting or temper tantrums to get their own way. They have difficulty sharing or working together because of selfishness. As a result, they have little self-control in their words and actions. Aggressive people give a false sense of importance and strength. In reality, they are weak inside and have a low self-esteem. They have a fear that no one listens, or understands them. Their unreasonable approach to others results in their fears being realized. This exaggerated sense of importance causes them to use their voice in a loud way to get their point across.

> John was an angry man who had been deeply hurt by an over-controlling father. He had much insecurity, especially about his worth as a person. All these factors would come out when he was angry, which was often. One could hear his voice going up with demands for strict obedience. Any resistance was met with an even louder voice until it seemed he would explode. Everyone around him lived in fear of his temper and resented him for it. He lost the relationships with his children and wife. He had no friends. Simply put, aggressive anger controlled his life. It was sad to watch. Only later in life did he realize his mistake and modify his aggressive anger.

While this may seem like an extreme example, the pain caused by aggressive anger, even if less pronounced, is profound. There is a feeling by others that they are being misused by this person.

The various types of aggressive anger are:

Constant anger. Because of great inner hurt, these people feel threats from everyone. Thus, they project constant anger to keep others away, which makes them think they are safe. They usually have unrealistic beliefs and great frustration. Because they feel so inadequate, they fear revealing their inner selves. They seek constant control of others through their anger. Consequently, relationships are non-existent, or very limited. They are usually very pessimistic about their lives. Underneath, these people are very unhappy but safe, they think. Andrew Lestor in his book, *Coping with Your Anger,* describes constant anger as: "These people relate angrily because they feel constantly threatened on every front."

Explosive anger is when anger erupts in destructive physical violence. Usually this occurs because they were scared as a child. As adults, they spread their hurt on others around them—both physically and emotionally. The victims feel as if they are being used for someone else's expense. Control is achieved by physical means and seems absolute. The victims feel such strong resentment that they bear scars for life unless major therapy is undertaken successfully. Relationships are destroyed as victims seek to flee from this painful aggression. The sad part is that victims oftentimes inflict this type of anger on others once they get older.

Misplaced anger: when we get angry at someone who is a powerful person in our lives (like a parent) or an authority figure (like a boss). The person's position prevents us from taking direct action against the original person who has hurt us. As a result, we take our anger out on an innocent third party, who is usually weaker and non-threatening. The third party can also be an inanimate object like a wall, or window. This is what my son did in the example at the beginning of this book. It's like the proverbial story about the boss making me so angry I go home and kick the dog. This action creates great resentment in the innocent party (people if not animals) because they don't understand why they are being hurt. Misplaced anger fails to deal directly with the original problem so it fails to resolve the problem. Fear of confrontation with the original authority prevents resolution. Misplaced anger yields only temporary pleasure, but fails long-term. This anger will damage or destroy relationships with children.

An evaluation of this form of anger:

Respect for others—very little, if any. Self-centered.

Relationships—limited, actually damages relationships of others around this person. Has few close friends. Children fear the person.

Control—seeks strong control of others but has poor self-control.

Frustrations—people don't hear or understand the person's increasing anger.

Emotional maturity—childlike behavior with little growth. "I want my way."

Long-term effect—their children may adopt this form of anger as they grow up. They become more isolated from others.

Overall effectiveness of this type—fails in all the above aspects. The message is not received and resentment builds in others. This behavior results in greater anger among everyone involved.

Is this your type of expressing anger? Are you happy with the results? Are all parties happy with the results? If not, would you like to change?

PASSIVE-AGGRESSIVE ANGER

Passive-aggressive anger uses subtle means of expressing anger as opposed to the openness of aggressive anger. People with this type of anger have a hidden disrespect for others as they want to hurt them in a quiet non-cooperative way. They outwardly deny that they are angry and often believe that themselves. This is because they are really fearful of anger and openness. However, their actions reflect a quiet hostility and evasiveness that tell the real story. This type of anger generates, over time, angry reactions from others once the targets of this behavior realize what has happened. The passive-aggressive person tries to entice the other person into aggressive anger. When the aggressor reacts, the passive provoker feels superior for not showing aggressive anger. In his book, *The Anger Trap,* Dr. Les Carter states: "They reason that if they do not fully disclose the nature of their anger, others cannot easily control or overpower them." They don't get openly angry, but want to get revenge.

Because of the denial feature, passive-aggressive anger is difficult to correct; openness is required for real correction. Many times, once one person starts using passive-aggressive anger, the receiving person will resort to the same type of anger with no resolution being reached. Christians are prone to use passive-aggressive anger, because they mistakenly use only the Bible verses that speak against anger. The Bible does, however, speak against the concept of revenge in Leviticus 19:18: *"Do not seek revenge or bear a grudge against one of your people, but love your neighbor as yourself. I am the Lord."*

The equation for passive-aggressive anger is:

Fear of Openness → threat → anxiety → passive-aggressive anger → No resolution. Pain continues. Others angry at us.

The fear of being open controls this person so that he uses passive-aggressive anger. In other words, he or she feels unable, or lacks the confidence, to express anger in an open way. This lack of action reflects a low self-esteem as he lacks the confidence to express his anger to get positive results.

In actuality, passive-aggressive people have a stronger desire to control their environment than aggressive people. This control is vital to the passive person to avoid being forthright and open. By being vague and unclear they are able to manipulate the situation to their own self-interest. Because of this self-preoccupation, they have problems with a God who has clear rules.

Passive-aggressive anger shows itself in many forms as:

Hostile silence. This may seem like a misnomer. A person with this type of anger will sometimes stop talking entirely to another person because of the anger they feel. This action reflects a deep-rooted hostility, hence the term "hostile anger," which I created. Andrew Lestor in *Coping with Your Anger* states: "Silence and withdrawal are two of the most common means by which persons try to conceal anger, yet make sure their displeasure is known."

Hostile silence shows no respect for the other person as it appears as if the other person doesn't exist. The passive-aggressive person is uncomfortable with open aggressive anger because he sees its negative effects. Therefore, this type of anger may result in both parties withdrawing to mutually hostile corners. This type of situation may go on for a long time until one of the parties breaks the silence with openness. Christians often adopt this type of anger expression since it avoids the "unchristian aggressive anger." It seems like an acceptable way of expressing anger and still remain a "nice" Christian. In reality, the opposite is true because the anger builds up inside creating bitterness, which is a sin. Paul tells us in Ephesians 4:31; *"Get rid of all bitterness . . ."*

> Ellen grew up with an aggressively angry father. Disliking this form of anger, she chose to adopt passive-aggressive anger. She felt comfortable with this choice. Her favorite tactic was to use hostile silence when angry. Everyone in her family would just know when Ellen was angry. She soon discovered that she could control her environment using this behavior. In fact, she found hostile silence to be very effective until she got married. When her husband refused to accept it, she sought help and later changed.

Purposely doing a poor job. There is intent to punish the other person, or authority by purposely not doing what is expected. Some examples are doing only half the job, or doing it late. People with anger may work at half-speed or slower. This action serves to purposely antagonize the authority or other person. They act irresponsibly and can't be counted on for important assignments. These actions all lead to great frustration in the receiving party, which leads them to get angry. There is, however, no resolution until the parties face the problems openly. Being consistently late, or procrastinating on returning phone calls or meetings can be another sign of this type of anger. This action may be used particularly when the person realizes that the other party likes punctuality. There is a demonstrated lack of care for the other person's desires. They secretly seek to actively antagonize.

Complaining or nagging: appears to have a desire to help someone, but underneath is a message of control and frustration. Andrew Lester in his book, *Coping with Your Anger,* describes nagging as ". . . reveals long-standing anger in response to the threat of powerlessness." Nagging may be masked as a "I-want-to-help-you" message. However, the receiver will realize that the real reason is a desire to control them and/or their actions. The receiver senses the disrespect and will want to take counter action including anger. Nagging and complaining can be damaging to relationships because of the way control is exerted.

> Betty, a long-term Christian, would use hostile silence and angry stares to control other people with her anger. This combination seemed to enable her to get her way. In fact, many times she was known to continue these negative actions for months. She thought that this tactic was better as a Christian since it wasn't the sin of explosive anger. However, those receiving this disrespectful treatment felt resentment and would stay away from her. Even some of her friends felt coldness from her in their interactions. She began to wonder why people were staying distant and realized that this anger form was counterproductive. After examining what was happening, she decided to give up this form of anger and felt better.

Being constantly forgetful or making mistakes: a forgetfulness that is consistent. Unless there is a physical reason, this seems innocent. Yet, its repetition over time will cause someone to finally realize that passive-aggressive anger is being expressed.

Purposely evasive in their commitments and responsibilities. They mistakenly perceive that anyone calling them to a meeting or to take on a responsibility is controlling them. They don't understand their right to free choice, but they fear the honesty of saying "no." Consequently, they will just not show up or notify someone that they are not coming. Their own needs dominate their thoughts and actions to the detriment of others.

The following is an evaluation of passive-aggressive anger:

Respect for others—little respect for the feelings of others. Self-absorbed.

Relationship—limited to a few superficial friends.

Control—wants strong control. Personal freedom and different ideas are not acknowledged. Others feel resentment.

Frustrations—those who practice this anger are not appreciated for accomplishments, because of others' resentments. As a result, frustration grows.

Emotional maturity—limited, because self-concern dominates; not others-directed, like Jesus wants us to be.

Long-term effect—people recognize this behavior and dislike it.

In summary, passive-aggressive anger fails in all categories. It creates greater anger. It may have short-term effectiveness for the user, but fails in the long-term. It is the most difficult form of anger to change.

Is this your type of anger expression? Are you happy with the results? Would you like to change your anger expression?

HOLDING IN ANGER

Holding anger in is sometimes called storing or stuffing anger. Instead of expressing anger, we hold it inside ourselves. People mistakenly think that by hiding the pain inside that it will just go away. They are fearful of open anger, because of the bad result(s) they have seen or felt. After a while, however, anger held in changes and reappears as aggressive anger. Since anger is a form of energy, which held inside becomes like a pressure cooker, it can't be contained forever. Eventually there is an explosion of anger for a minor reason usually, at the wrong time and the wrong place. In the book, *Design For Wholeness,* by Loughlan Sofield ST, Sister Carroll Juliano SHCJ and Sister Rosine Hammett, the authors write: "There is energy created by anger, however, and that energy has to have an outlet. Anger that is continually stored is a destructive option. It has serious consequences in that it destroys both the person and relationships." Consequently, people who store their anger have a problem with it exploding into aggressive anger because of bottled-up energy. People with this form of anger usually keep account of all the wrongs done to them by a person. Thus, resolution of anger held in does not happen. The book further states: "This will result in a variety of illnesses such as heart attack, stroke, ulcers and high blood pressure. In this case stored anger can actually kill you."

Many times, these people hold not only their anger inside, but their other emotions as well. They fear others will not accept them with all their emotions. Additionally, they are reluctant to admit their own personal problems. This secretiveness makes it difficult to develop close relationships. They even try to hide their anger from themselves through constant denial. Avoiding problem situations is important to people with this type of anger as they can be controlled by aggressive angry people. This occurrence only serves to make them feel more disrespected and insignificant. Frequently they struggle with inferiority and resentment feelings which negatively affect their self-worth.

The equation for held in anger is:

> **Fear of exposure → Threat → Anxiety → Stored Anger →
> No resolution. Pain continues. Others angry with us.**

Some evidences of this behavior are:

Withdrawal from angry situations. They fear the conflict more than finding a solution that will better both parties. As a result, they will have a compulsive desire to avoid/flee from angry situations.

Trying to be pleasant to everyone. This people-pleasing technique fails. Some people still won't like them even after all that they have tried to please them. People using stored anger pretend to be people they think they should be rather than who they are. Accordingly, they are not real persons.

Fail to stand for unpopular positions. Because they fear the anger of others, they lack the courage to stand for what is right, or even godly. Consequently, they may struggle with evangelism, because of the potential rejection involved.

Generally, they are pessimistic about relationships and the world. They don't feel valued for themselves when things don't work out. Their inability to face the person making them angry makes them prone to depression and self-hatred.

They are prone to lie about their feelings and anger. Therefore, they would rather lie than face the truth. Openness is scary and to be avoided. Denial and/or evasiveness control the actions of a person with stored anger.

Boredom. This may be a more acceptable anger expression for some Christian people. In *Design For Wellness* the authors state that boredom is an accepted emotion: "Boredom is masked anger." Christian people may change their anger expression to a more acceptable expression for anger like boredom. They may become depressed from anger turned inward. In both cases, Christians are seeking acceptable ways of expressing their anger albeit a negative anger expression.

> Fred had been a NYC bus driver before he entered Syracuse Teen Challenge. Outwardly he had a quiet pleasant personality. Nothing, he boasted, could outwardly make him angry. He was very content with storing his anger. I warned him that he needed to deal with the anger building up inside or his anger would become aggressive anger. Day after day, he continued holding his anger in and he appeared to be succeeding. Then one day his built-up anger suddenly changed into rage. He, in fact, almost physically hurt another person in the program. At that point, he sought help for his anger.

The following is an evaluation of stuffing anger:

Respect for others—overly respectful to other's feelings and submerging their own feelings. Others see this and may not be respectful back.

Relationships—limited to surface relationships since they fear exposing their true feelings.

Control—have little and are controlled by others. Tries to control others by being "nice."

Frustrations—why can't others just love me since I am so nice to them? Why can't I find happiness?

Emotional maturity—low, since they are still childlike. Lack the maturity to be open and honest about their feelings.

Long-term effect—feeling isolated and alone often. Not able to grapple with the difficulties of living with others.

In summary, holding in anger also fails to resolve anger and leaves the person feeling negative about himself. They believe in the illusion that "out- of-sight-out-of-mind," which never works.

Is this your type of anger expression? Are you happy with the results? Would you like to change your anger expression?

It should be noted that some people may use two types of negative anger depending on the situation. This action may take the form of passive-aggressive anger and aggressive anger. Such an unusual combination is the result of fear of directly facing a particular person because of that person's type of anger, or their position of authority.

> Amy usually expressed aggressive anger in most angry situations. However, with her husband she found his strong aggressive anger was too difficult to face. Seeking a more successful way of expressing her anger, she changed to using passive-aggressive anger with her husband. This change seemed to work for her. At least she wasn't getting blasted by her husband as when she aggressively confronted him. However, over time, the new anger approach also failed.

Despite these negative results, some people still cling to negative anger. They see secondary gains from it, which may occur for a short term. Thus, they hold onto negative anger for some of the following reasons:

1. To protect themselves from an inner insecurity. People are so fearful of exposing their inner selves that they put up a façade of anger. Also, people mistakenly feel that they are so guilty or unworthy that no one would accept them. People think that their sins are unforgivable.

2. Keep them from feeling more painful emotions, like loneliness, abuse, great losses or sadness. The pain of these emotions is greater than any pain the anger might cause. As a result, they logically seek the lesser pain.

3. Fear of intimacy. They are afraid of relationships so they use constant aggressive anger to keep people away. This action is successful on one level, but the person pays a terrible price. They will feel great loneliness as there is a hunger for intimate relationships in all of us.

4. To get attention. Such actions as pouting, sulking, shouting and tirades can be cries for attention, or control. This childlike behavior, if used into adult years, becomes a problem in relationships as others feel controlled by it.

> Sandy needed to be the center of attention to build her self-esteem. She would use jokes or stories to control conversations for long periods. These actions became irritating to others who sought a more balanced give-and-take in conversations. She continued this controlling behavior, but wondered why people would avoid her. Finally to her astonishment, a friend told her about the distastefulness of her controlling actions. This action caused Sandy to tone down her self-centered desire for attention and find emotional peace.

5. Depression. Can be caused from turning anger inward, which can seem like a lifeless existence. Consequently, expressing aggressive anger outward can be a way of giving the person a feeling of new energy.

While all these misplaced expressions of anger may provide fleeting gains, they disappear over time. Often, these types of behavior also tend to isolate the person more. Relationships are damaged and love feelings toward the person are reduced.

At Teen Challenge we have found that negative anger can have that same power as drugs on a man. This bondage of negative anger in men's lives has caused men not only to hurt others, but also to harm themselves with drugs. Thus, we find that true healing takes time as they work through their anger with God's help.

As we have seen, all three negative expressions of anger (aggressive, passive aggressive and storing) fail badly in dealing with anger. Instead, anger (pain) develops in others, because basic biblical principles for resolution are missing. As a result, I call negative anger—a path to pain. Usually the anger cycle of negative anger inciting negative anger continues until someone changes, or finds a positive anger expression. The main problem is that we don't know, or we haven't been taught, how to express our anger in a positive way.

Did you see your type of expressed anger described above? Have you felt frustrated at the results of your anger?

I personally have felt the utter frustration of searching for a positive way to express anger. My problem was that I was only aware of the negative ways. No one for years ever told me, or modeled for me positive anger. Accordingly, for years, I clung to stuffing my anger with negative results. Finally, I began to learn about positive anger. I fully realize that most people only know and use the three negative anger expressions. They feel caught and frustrated with constant failure. In the next chapter, we shall present handling anger in a positive way that has worked for me and many others for over a decade.

Summary:

1. Aggressive anger—hitting, shouting and using physical force to express anger. Characteristics: don't listen to others, give unwanted advice, act like children and have a false sense of importance.

2. Types of aggressive anger—constant, explosive and misplaced.

3. Passive-aggressive anger—expresses anger subtly not openly. Characteristics: denial feature making this anger the most difficult to correct.

4. Types of passive-aggressive anger—hostile silence, purposely doing a poor job, purposely late, nagging, constantly forgetful and evasive.

5. Holding anger in—evidences are: withdrawal from angry situations, trying to be pleasant to everyone, failure to stand for unpopular positions, generally pessimistic about relationships and the world, prone to lie about their feelings of anger and boredom.

Discussion Questions

1. What are the three types of negative anger expressions?

2. Which negative anger expression do (did) you often use? What were your results?

3. In what ways is negative anger a bondage in your life?

4. Have you ever used more than one negative anger expression? If so, which ones?

Chapter 3
Anger Reconciliation:
A Way to Harmony

I have purposely titled this book, *Anger Reconciliation,* which, at first glance, seems like an odd pairing of words that should not go together. Others have told me that I should use the title: "Anger Management." Those words to me, however, imply that we are just controlling our anger, not resolving it, or using it for a good purpose. With God's direction, I have purposely chosen the word "reconciliation" to point toward the goal of harmony and peace for all of our angry situations. The definition of reconciliation is: "to restore to friendship, compatibility or harmony."

Imagine being angry with someone and ending up having a sense of harmony or peace with that person after talking it out. Jesus tells us in Matthew 5:24: "*. . . First go and be reconciled to your brother . . .*" After teaching my class on anger for several years, I read this verse and it showed me a deeper meaning from Christ: I needed to go further than forgive my brother—I needed to reconcile with him. True reconciliation (peace) should be the goal every time we have an angry situation with someone. Through reconciliation we can break the bondage of negative anger. Anger reconciliation enables me to change my perception of anger from an adversarial relationship to one where understanding and even greater intimacy can develop.

This book is a product of my studying about anger from such books as: The Bible, *The Soul Care Bible, The Anger Workbook, Coping with Your Anger, Man to Man, The Anger Trap, Mad About Us, The Dance of Anger, Making Peace With Conflict, Boundaries, Design for Wholeness, Anger is a Choice* and numerous Christian articles on anger. Also teaching about anger over 14 years at Teen Challenge, I have found that Satan is only involved in one anger expression (negative) while God wants us to express one of three positive expressions.

In negative anger, lies and discord are prevalent. Much of the pain in negative anger comes from dissension and lack of peace. In effect, we are out of God's plan and Satan is in charge. Personally, I have found positive anger expression accomplishes the following positive results:

- **Positive anger creates opportunities for deeper personal and interpersonal growth.**

- **Positive anger helps resolve problems without leaving resentment.**

- **Positive anger respects each party in the angry situation.**

- **Positive anger changes hostility to harmony (peace) as the ideal result.**

Over the years my study, prayer and reading about anger have helped me to change my mind and emotions regarding my previous habit of responding with negative anger and storing it. To achieve positive anger responses and reconciliation to conflicts, I have found some biblical principles that are necessary to follow:

1. Bring God into our anger situation through prayer. Most people don't even think God is concerned about their anger. If He is, they think, He should just get rid of it for us. Yet, like many difficult situations, God often doesn't relieve us of the trial, but rather takes us through it. He does this because He has a lesson in it for us. It stands to reason, if God cares about something as insignificant as a hair on my head (Luke 21:18), He really cares about how I express my anger. Through His guidance, God wants to show you and I how to express our anger positively. Formerly, I depended upon my experience and my own mind to handle angry situations. These actions, unfortunately, never resolved my anger. Through God's miraculous intervention in our anger situations, however, we can achieve breakthroughs and peace. Thus it is critical that we always bring God into our conflicts.

One of the best examples of God responding to a prayer at the moment of conflict occurred during one of my classes at Syracuse Teen Challenge.

> Murray got up with his fists clenched and stated, "I'm angry with Don and I need to talk with him." As the teacher of the 'Anger Reconciliation' class at Syracuse Teen Challenge, I could see that a fist fight was coming between Murray and Don. I told Murray that he must pray before he talked to Don. This he did. When he finished, his fists were not clenched. He went over to Don and started talking and Don immediately apologized. They shook hands and the matter was resolved for both parties. The class clapped and congratulated Murray. I stopped them and pointed out to everyone how the prayer to God had made the difference. Murray agreed with me. Prayer is the most important part of the positive anger process. God can change our tendency from using negative anger to using positive anger with productive results.

In negative anger expression, prayer is almost never used. In fact, many times God's name is disrespected and used as a swear word. Sometimes we can pray selfishly just to get our own way. The results are predictably painful.

2. Show Respect. Respect is defined as: "that we show high regard or concern for someone." This means that I show love or care for the other person. At a deeper level, respect can mean the desire to understand someone and be understood. We all hunger for that type of relationship. I have found that showing respect toward the other person in an angry situation is usually the opposite from what they expect. Thus, respect is critical in changing the normal negative dynamics of anger to a more positive atmosphere.

Dr. Les Carter writes in his book, *Anger Trap*, the importance of respect as follows: "... they recognize that life consists of an ongoing series of exchanges that can produce either increased friction or an atmosphere of respect. Their priority is to seek the path toward mutual respect."

The Bible also mentions the importance of respecting one another in a number of verses. 1 Peter 2:17 states: *"Show proper respect to everyone: Love the brotherhood of believers..."* Jesus commanded us to *"love your neighbor as yourself"* (Matt. 19:19). This verse tells me that we are to be loving toward someone who may even have hurt us. God asks us to reject the usual human reaction of revenge because the Bible states: *"Do not take revenge, my friends, but leave room for God's wrath, for it is written: 'It is mine to avenge; I will repay,' says the Lord"*(Romans 12:19).

I have discovered that when I show the other person respect they will tend to reflect respect back to me. Usually the first words I express in my anger, and how I express them, sets the tone for the eventual result. Respect, therefore, is crucial and must be shown from the very beginning when trying to resolve an angry situation. In my anger interactions, I try to express life-giving words in a life-giving way. The exact details of showing step-by-step respect when dealing with anger are described later in this chapter under the section RAA.

In negative anger, respect is almost always missing in words, tone of voice and actions. This is probably the most pronounced difference between the two types of anger.

3. Acknowledge the freedom of others to make their own choices. This means I need to respect differences of opinion between myself and others. God gives us freedom of choice, but as Christians we have a responsibility to: 1) not indulge in sin 2) not cause others to sin 3) serve others. Galatians 5:13 confirms this: *"You, my brothers were called to be free. But do not use your freedom to indulge the sinful nature; rather serve one another in love."* I serve others by accepting differences between myself and others. People often try to force us into their conformity. God created differences between us for a positive purpose. He wants us to value differences as long they are not violating biblical principles. Differences provide us with many new and exciting ways of thinking and acting. I have felt resentment when other people have tried to control my thoughts and/or actions without my approval.

In negative anger, freedom of choice is consistently denied as conformity and control of other people's opinions are the norm. Also personal differences are not accepted, but rejected.

4. Have an optimistic outlook. I have discovered that when I put my trust in God, He will help heal our hurts and problems. He will guide us with positive anger to help us resolve our anger issues. Trusting God gives us a hope that a real resolution of these issues will be achieved. Proverbs 3:5-6 highlights this: *"Trust in the Lord with all your heart and lean not on your own understanding; in all your ways acknowledge him and he will make your paths straight."* Through trusting the Lord, I may have successful anger resolution, or at least a peace in my soul. Trusting God results in our whole outlook becoming optimistic.

On the other hand, those expressing negative anger tend to be pessimists. They have experienced such pain and alienation from the results of their anger that they tend to see their world as a dark place with little hope.

5. Establish a dialogue with the other person. Dialogue is defined "as the successful verbal open exchange of ideas and feelings between two or more people." To be successful, I find dialogue requires both of us to talk, listen and try to mutually understand the other's position. To accomplish this may take time. I have discovered that dialogue requires us to reveal some of our inner selves and show concern for the other's thoughts and feelings. In the book, *Design for Wholeness,* the authors express the value of dialogue this way: "Dialogue moves a relationship from dependence to interdependence, to a sense of belonging and bonding to the life-giving relationships for which humans were created."

The process of reaching a mutual understanding may seem

impossible to us in an angry situation. During an argument, however, our purpose is not to get the other person to agree with us, but to understand the other person. If the two of us can agree to disagree in this case, we can maintain mutual respect. I have found that the most painful incidents of anger occur with those I know the best. Accordingly, it is important to learn to effectively dialogue in those familiar situations. Unfortunately, in other angry situations, such as with strangers or authority figures, real dialogue may be more difficult or impossible. I shall discuss some steps to help create effective dialogue later in Chapter Five.

In negative anger expression, dialogue doesn't exist. There is little attempt to listen or understand the other person. The main desire is to use negative anger to force or manipulate your ideas on the other person. In other words, the need to dominate takes priority over relating to the other person, which makes mutual understanding impossible.

6. Develop Emotional maturity. God wants us to mature both emotionally and spiritually. In Hebrews 5:14 maturity is expressed: *"But solid food is for the mature, who by constant use have trained themselves to distinguish good from evil."* This verse tells us that knowing good from evil is critical for making mature decisions. Also, maturity comes from my taking responsibility for how I express my anger in a way that benefits both parties. If I currently use negative anger, I may have felt God leading me to consider more positive alternatives. When I have taken responsibility for my anger expression, I have sought God's plan using these principles as listed. When I did this, I began to use positive anger expression and I experienced growth emotionally and spiritually. Emotional maturity, I believe, is: believing in your own worth, expressing emotions in a respectful assertive way, handling your anger constructively and having an optimistic spirit to overcome difficulties. I develop the topic of maturity in a deeper way in Chapter Seven: "Taking Responsibility for My Anger."

In negative anger there is a childlike irresponsibility or stubbornness. Emotional maturity is not sought so growth is stagnated.

7. Grow in Patience. Patience is defined as: "The capacity to endure evil, adversity or pain with fortitude." Proverbs 14:29 also says: *"A patient man has great understanding, but a quick-tempered man displays folly."* I have found that using patience is a necessity in reaching a resolution for angry situations. We all want to be understood by others and this requires our patience, not folly. Therefore, patience is listed as a fruit of the Holy Spirit in Galatians 5:22. I show loving care for someone when I don't push my desires on them with hostile words, a high volume of words, and a display of impatience. This loving spirit becomes evident to the other person and creates a much greater opportunity for dialogue.

With negative anger expression, there is an impatience and lack of mutual understanding. Other people feel pushed by our selfish rush to get our own way. This action creates resistance in others, which of course, further tests our patience. Thus by rushing and being impatient, we get the opposite results of what we seek. The old adage, "slow down and you'll go faster," applies here.

8. Seek the truth in our angry situations. Many times lies and/or misunderstandings are the source of many arguments. God wants us to live in the truth and remove the lies that bind us. Ephesians 6:14 tells us to daily: *"Stand firm then, with the belt of truth buckled around your waist . . ."* Truth will prevent the lies of Satan from controlling us. The principle of living in the truth, as set forth in the book, *Boundaries,* by Dr. Henry Cloud and Dr. John Townsend, states: "There is always safety in the truth, whether it be knowing God's truth or knowing the truth about yourself." This safety protects us from the painful consequences of living in lies.

I have found that some people have tried to implant lies into my life with ungodly values. These lies, once believed, have resulted in my being controlled by them. An example of this was my father advising me to only associate with important people so I could get ahead in the world. Later, upon finding the truth that God wants me to associate with all people, I found greater peace in my life. By using "theophastic prayer," Jesus released lies in my life that bound me by revealing His truth, which gave me peace (for details on Theophastic Prayer Ministry see Chapter 4). Also believing lies can make us unjustly angry with people.

In negative anger, lies and discord are prevalent. Much of the pain in negative anger comes from dissension and lack of peace. In effect, we are out of God's plan and Satan is in charge. Putting all these principles together, there are three positive anger options:

I. RIGHTEOUS ANGER

Righteous anger deals with the ungodly actions and injustices in this world. God tells us to get angry over these situations. Jesus used this righteous anger to physically clear the temple of the money changers (John 2:13-17) "*. . . Jesus went up to Jerusalem. In the temple courts he found men selling cattle, sheep and doves, and others sitting at tables exchanging money. So he made a whip out of cords, and drove all from the temple area, both sheep and cattle; he scattered the coins of the money changers and overturned their tables. To those who sold doves he said, 'Get these out of here! How dare you turn my Father's house into a market!'* "

We see the zeal of Jesus to cleanse the temple of sinful business where it should be solely a place of worship. The fact that Jesus used physical force and strong words to accomplish this demonstrates His seriousness about this situation. It is a lesson to all of us that sometimes God may want us to get angry at sin that violates God's biblical principles. In *Coping with Your Anger* Andrew Lester states: "Jesus, like all humans got angry. However, he did not sin with his anger! His anger was mobilized in the service of love as he protested superficial religion and acted out of God's displeasure."

Righteous anger also occurs when our deeply felt values are violated. When this happens, righteous anger is a call to action to correct what we believe is wrong. As long as I observe the Christian means of expressing my anger (positive anger), righteous anger is constructive to all of us and society (i.e. the reduction of: racism, abortion, prejudice etc.) God's word motivates us to correct injustices in our lives and/ or society. Too often, we Christians don't feel righteous anger in our lives toward these injustices in our nation because of our distaste for expressing anger. We need to feel angry when we see human freedoms diminished by ungodly actions. Through righteous anger we demonstrate true Christian love for others. The equation for righteous anger is:

God's Precepts → injustice or attack on our values → anxiety → righteous anger → society changed; personal values upheld

> My wife and I were unable to have children. Accordingly we tried to adopt an infant, which was difficult as some agencies thought I was too old at 38. This rejection created righteous anger in me about abortion. Later, we were blessed to adopt an infant son. Sensing the injustice of the abortion issue, my wife and I, with our two-year-old son, would attend anti-abortion rallies at Planned Parenthood. Holding my son on my shoulders, we would march and pray there. We would hold up signs saying, "Adoption Not Abortion." My righteous anger against abortion continues today.

Evaluating righteous anger in the following categories:

Respect for others—depending on the severity of the injustice, respect for others may be subordinated and reduced to insure that there is a change of the injustice. More recent forms of righteous anger have shown more respect for others' rights (i.e. marches and boycotts). We all remember how Martin Luther King's marches and speeches touched the heart of the nation and helped eliminate the injustice of racial discrimination. Respecting God's principles in these situations is more important than others' rights. Others see righteous anger succeeding in achieving positive changes, which over time, they respect.

Relationships—initially they may be fractured due to the need to institute change. Later upon reflection, others may be drawn to relationship as they see the societal benefits. By being forthright with our values, others see us as real people who are not afraid to stand for what they feel is right. This courage is sorely needed in our society today.

Control—God is in control when correcting injustice. We need to use godly ways to achieve major changes in the culture. Calling on the Holy Spirit, we can stand strong for our closely-held values.

Frustrations—change does not happen quickly, particularly significant social change. Thus, it can seem frustrating to us. Also, the tactics used to create change may frustrate others. Our stand for our values may frustrate others for a while.

Emotional maturity—from God's perspective—is very high. He has a calling for all of us to correct injustice. Self-esteem is strengthened when we stand up for our values.

Long-term effect—will be the best for everyone. There may be, however, lingering resentments with some of the people who resisted change. People see us as committed people when we stand by our valued principles.

In summary, righteous anger has mostly positive benefits for all. This occurs because God is behind such changes. Our characters will be stronger when we stand up for our godly values and we may well provoke others to examine and change their own deeply held convictions.

William Wilberforce, of the 18th century, who finally convinced Parliament to abolish slavery after 20 years, is another prime example of righteous anger. Also, those standing against sexual slavery today.

II. RELEASING ANGER

Can also be described as ways to let go of our anger. In any event, the anger (energy) feelings are dissipated as a way of dealing with them.

This is accomplished when we do either of the following:

1. Dropping anger. I am unable to express anger because of certain uncontrollable limitations on my life such as: income taxes, stop lights, societal rules, etc. While I don't like being controlled by these restrictions, I alone can't change them. Consequently, I find it is pointless to get angry with them. I just have to accept these types of restrictions on my life. However, when these rules become unjust, then righteous anger may be necessary to change them.

2. Forgiveness. I don't want to assert my anger because I realize that the matter is minor, or I want to forgive the other person. Forgiveness is defined as: "a process of ceasing to feel resentment against someone or to pardon someone." Jesus confirms the importance of forgiveness in Matthew 6:14: *"For if you forgive men when they sin against you, your heavenly Father will also forgive you. But, if you do not forgive men of their sins, your Father will not forgive your sins."* Therefore, forgiveness is one of Christianity's greatest callings for all of us. In *Design for Wholeness* the authors state: "The choice to forgive brings with it a feeling of relief, a freedom of spirit and renewed life. It is often the one who forgives rather than the person who is forgiven who receives the greater benefit." Consequently, we see the spiritual and emotional importance of forgiveness to each of us. I have found that forgiveness requires my personal commitment to rid myself of a desire for retaliation and revenge. Personally, I have discovered that while I might forgive someone, I also need to pray for them. This action allows the Holy Spirit to accomplish complete forgiveness.

The equation for releasing anger is:

**Biblical understanding → threat → anxiety →
dropping anger; forgiveness → resolution for every one**

As an example of the power of forgiveness, I experienced the following:

> Returning home in my car, I suddenly noticed a car had come out of a side road just in front of me and was blocking both lanes of the road. This act left me with no place to go except off the road. I tried to do this, but the other car was too close and I felt the crash as we hit. My car went off the road and into a field. I was not severely hurt but I did have pain in my chest and knee. My car, however, was totaled. Later, as we were both lying on boards in the ambulance going to the hospital, the driver of the other car apologized to me for running the stop sign. She asked me to forgive her. Still suffering physically from what she had done, I hesitated as I still felt anger at her for causing the accident. Finally, I realized my responsibility as a Christian and forgave her. Afterward, I felt a peace as my anger left me.

Asking for and giving forgiveness frees both parties of the potential of bitterness. We shall discuss forgiveness in a deeper way in Chapter 7.

One of the big dangers with dropping anger is that we may deceive ourselves that we have done it when, in reality, we may have just stored it. I have found that the real test is not to keep a mental ledger of the anger situations with the other person. Confession of our anger to God is the best way to release it. If, after going to God, we still hold resentment, then we are still storing anger. At this point, we may consider Christian counseling since the incident that evoked the resentment may only be a trigger to a previous experience that we have not yet resolved.

Evaluating "releasing anger" in the following categories:

Respect for others—very high, because we consider the feelings of others.

Relationships—are stronger as long as there is no stuffing or storing of anger.

Control—demonstrates control over anger. We don't seek control over the other person.

Frustrations—none as long as the anger is truly dropped/forgiven.

Emotional maturity—is very high. Shows care for others.

Long-term effect—there are no negative effects. With forgiveness, there will be resolution for all parties.

In summary, releasing anger shows concern for the other person through forgiveness. It also demonstrates self-control over our anger, which has positive effects on others.

III. RESPECTFUL ASSERTIVE ANGER

Respectful Assertive Anger (RAA) is a new anger expression incorporating the biblical principles listed above. Over three years, God helped me to develop RAA after Bible reading on anger and reconciliation, and prayer to find the godly way to express my anger. For material on dealing with anger in a Christian way, I read 11 Christian books on anger (see bibliography at back of book). None of them had a similar concept to RAA, except one, which mentioned reflection. Accordingly, most of the steps of RAA were developed from Scripture and from my classes with the students at Syracuse and Orlando Teen Challenge centers. RAA creates an atmosphere that leads to dialogue and reconciliation of our anger, which helps us to build our relationships. By using RAA, we are able to set limits on others who are violating us in some significant way. RAA is the anger expression that we can all use successfully for most of our anger situations. Over the last 14 years, I have found, as well as many of my students who have used this method, resolution for our angry conflicts.

RAA starts with **R for respectful**. I find that I must first respect God through prayer about my anger. He cares very much about my anger and how I express it. I have discovered that seeking God's wisdom is the MOST important step I can take to express my anger in a positive way. For RAA to be successful, I find it necessary to pray to God for the following:

Peace. The definition is: "a mental or spiritual condition marked by freedom from disquieting or oppressive thoughts or emotions." I have found that God is with us when we have peace vs. strife or discord. Jesus said in John 14:27: *"Peace I leave with you; my peace I give you . . ."* When some of us get angry, we allow our emotions to take control—especially aggressively angry people. Through prayer, however, God can calm our emotions down and give us peace. Then, we find that we are able to focus our mind, listen and understand what is happening in the upcoming dialogue. If after prayer, I still don't feel emotional peace, I don't quit, but I continue to pray for it. I've learned from experience that persistence does yield results and God will calm my emotions down if I keep at it.

Using the right words. I need to trust God to give me the life-giving words to say what will communicate respect to the other person. The words I use have great power. Most of us, when angry, seek revenge and use hurtful words reflecting our own hurt feelings. We need godly words that enable us to express our valid anger without creating anger in the other person. Positive words help create dialogue, which in turn leads to reconciliation of our anger. The need for using the right words is amplified in Proverbs 12:18: *"Reckless words pierce like a sword, but the tongue of the wise brings healing."* Also, in Proverbs 16:24: *"Pleasant words are a honeycomb, sweet to the soul and healing to the bones."* Specifically, I need to use "I" statements, not "you" statements. Like "I feel angry when you did . . ." This reflects my opinion. I ask questions as opposed to stating declarations. I also try to use caring words like, "I'm interested in your point of view," and, "I care for you." These kinds of words show my respect for the other person's opinion and a desire to engage them in dialogue.

How to speak our words. Many times, in our anger, we speak loudly as we try to enforce our will on the other person—especially true of aggressively angry people. This, however, offends the other person so that they don't want to hear us. To overcome this, I have found that Proverbs 15:1 *"A gentle answer turns away wrath, but a harsh word stirs up anger"* works in most cases (i.e. the example with my son at the beginning of this book. I told Andrew in a calm voice that he had to pay for and repair the door he had smashed). Many times using a quiet voice has the effect of bringing down the volume of the aggressively angry person. It is a way of showing respect for the other person. This does not mean that we are not firm in our speech, but in a quieter way. This way, of course, does require great patience and self-control when someone is shouting at us, but it will eventually work. If the other person continues to shout, stop and pray for peace (see the section on Time Out in Chapter 5).

> Edna was talking with her husband, Ed, about being disrespected by someone. She was shouting at Ed to get her point across. Ed calmly asked her to talk quietly to him, but she continued shouting with her emotions running high. When she wouldn't lower her voice, he said he wanted to pray. He asked her to pray, but she refused. Ed prayed quietly for peace. He tried to talk again, but Edna's emotions continued to dominate her. He went back to prayer. Still there was no success in reducing the volume of Edna's voice. Finally the third time the prayer worked and they had a productive dialogue when Ed empathized with her pain.

This real example demonstrates that patient prayer works.

For the other person to receive our words. I want the Holy Spirit to break down any walls that may exist which prevent the other person from receiving my words. There may be old negative feelings between myself and the other person. Satan uses negative situations to divide people. Therefore, I want God to help open the channel of dialogue between me and the other person so we can achieve mutual understanding.

While these are the prayers that I recommend, additional prayers, of course, can be added. Without prayers, I know from painful personal experience, RAA will not work because I have not asked God to intervene. I simply chose to rely on my own understanding to work out my anger instead of turning to God. Proverbs 3:5-6 applies here: "*Trust in the Lord with all your heart and lean not on your own understanding; In all your ways acknowledge him and he will make your paths straight.*"

The second part of R means to be respectful to the other person. Jesus said to "*love your neighbor as yourself*"(Matthew 19:19). We do this by "carefronting" vs. confronting the other person as used in negative anger. Confronting is defined as: "to stand facing or opposing esp. in challenge defiance, or accusation." As Christians we want to show more caring, which is why "carefronting" is better. "Carefronting" means caring for the other person by how I put into action the steps below.

A good question to ask ourselves regarding how we express our anger is: Do my actions reflect a godly way of dealing with this person?

Specifically this involves respecting the other person as follows:

Approach them calmly with a friendly manner. I recommend shaking their hand as a friendly gesture. Most people using negative anger will be hostile outwardly or subtly and want to stay distant.

Ask the other person if you can sit down. It is important to ask since this allows them to say no. If this happens then ask if the two of you could agree on another time to talk as you have something important to discuss. By sitting down, you are more at their level and less intimidating by not standing over them. This is particularly true with shorter people and children. Often times in negative anger situations, taller people will try to use their height to intimidate the other person. By making the physical stance more equal, I am more respectful. This point was suggested by a student at Syracuse Teen Challenge and we've used it ever since.

Ask the other person to pray together. This brings God's help into the coming discussion. If the other person does not want to pray or is an unbeliever, that is all right since you have already prayed.

The next letter of RAA **is A for assertive.** Assertive means "to state or affirm positively, assuredly, plainly or strongly." This means that I need to state calmly yet firmly my valid needs or values while respecting the dignity of the other person. Dr. Les Carter in the *Anger Trap* states: "Assertive people are firm in stating their convictions, yet that firmness is accompanied by the realization that others deserve to be given the room to decide for themselves how to respond." Assertiveness requires a delicate balance achieved by:

Thinking about the needs and feelings of the other person. Using life-giving words and giving the other person time to speak. Recognizing the other person by using phrases as "I care for you" or "I hope we can work this out" creates a connection with them. Everyone wants to feel that his or her feelings and thoughts are understood. This respectfulness usually will cause the other person to want to listen to you. In negative anger, the person will interrupt, use hostile words and ignore the other's feelings.

Staying calm but persistent. The calmness we show others, when discussing our anger, demonstrates respect and confidence in our desire to achieve resolution of our anger. Persistence may be necessary since we may be interacting with a person accustomed to expressing negative anger. As a result, their responses may be hostile and even anger baiting. We get this calmness and patience from our abiding in Christ. Negative anger can be both loud and irrational, or quiet and evasive.

Listening to what they are saying. Listening involves several levels of messages. What are they saying? How are they saying it? What do they really mean deep inside? This requires us to listen closely to what is said. The situation may require **reflective listening**—repeating back what you thought you heard from the other person. In effect, you are checking out what was said by that person. While it slows down the conversation, it can be crucial to truly understanding the other person. Reflective listening avoids misunderstandings from arising, which often happens with negative anger. When anger is expressed negatively, neither party is listening to the other, which only increases anger in both parties. Proverbs 19:20 points out the value of listening: *"Listen to advice and accept instruction, and in the end you will be wise."* If reconciliation is our goal, we must listen to the other person and try to understand them—even during a conflict.

Focusing on the other person and their body language. Eye contact is necessary to communicate your interest in the person as well as their importance. If your eyes wander, this communicates distraction and minimizes the value of your encounter to the receiver. Body language can also give hints to a person's real feelings although they can also be misinterpreted. For example, if someone has their fists clenched, this probably implies anger, while arms crossed in a blocking position may reflect anger, or could be just a comfortable position for the person. If you feel the other person's body language is telling you something about what they are feeling, ask them what they want to communicate. Men often will feel more comfortable by sending a message of anger through negative body language. In negative anger there will oftentimes be disrespectful body language gestures and actions that communicate anger, which may or may not be recognized or understood.

Keeping your hands at your side or visible. Hands moving around can create anxiety or tension. I found this is very important with the students at Syracuse Teen Challenge. They were concerned about their angry street experiences where other people would pull weapons out of their pockets. While that is not true for most of us, moving hands or pointing can be distracting. When in an angry situation people will often point their finger at the other person for emphasis or try to intimidate the other person.

Being brief and clear when expressing anger. I find it is very important that the other person understand clearly what I am angry about. I have seen many times in my "Teen Challenge Reconciliation" class where a student will not be clear about his anger, which creates confusion. Other times some students want to ramble on about their anger until the listener loses attention. This is what happens often with negative anger as the angry person keeps repeating the same points to justify his anger. The result is the listener gets frustrated and stops listening. Thus, real dialogue is lost. The importance of being clear is stated in Nehemiah 8:8: *"They read from the Book of the Law of God, making it clear and giving the meaning so that the people could understand what was being read."* The same is true when we speak clearly: people will understand us.

> Luis was angry at Bill in my "Anger Reconciliation Class" at Teen Challenge. Luis, while practicing RAA, kept going on and on about how Bill had made him so angry. After what seemed like a long time, Luis finally stopped talking. Bill looked at Luis and, in an agitated voice, said: "You talked so long I forgot what you were angry about." Luis, this time with more animation, started over again. I had to stop him and ask him to very briefly explain why he was angry with Bill. Luis seemed to understand, but still couldn't be brief. Finally, after witnessing other people being precise, Luis did better.

Seeking the truth. Sometimes we have heard that someone has gossiped about us, but, in reality, this may not be true. Therefore, finding the truth is critical to avoid misunderstandings. John 3:21 states: *"But whoever lives by the truth comes into the light, so that it may be seen plainly that what he has done has been done through God."* Finding the truth about an angry situation will lead to real peace in our lives. To do this, we may need to question the person and possible witnesses. With God's help, we shall discover the truth. Lies and distortions are prevalent with negative anger, which creates misunderstandings and no resolution.

Setting a boundary with the other person not to repeat the action that created the anger. I have discovered that setting a clear boundary is very important so that the other person doesn't repeat the same problem. The book, *Boundaries,* by Dr. Henry Cloud and Dr. John Townsend states: "Just as homeowners set physical property lines around their land, we need to set mental, physical, emotional and spiritual boundaries for our lives to help us distinguish what is our responsibility and what isn't." Accordingly, I need to clarify with others what is my responsibility and what is their responsibility. This clarity and respectful firmness reflects my convictions. The other person may disagree, but they know clearly where I stand. Lack of clear boundaries has many times led to continuing anger. If the fear of stating a boundary is a problem, ask God for strength. People will tend to respect boundaries when they are explained in a respectful way.

Being creative with new ideas that help to resolve problems. I have found this to be important when resolving angry situations. Sometimes, however, our way to correct an issue doesn't work with the other person. As a result, being patient and willing to explore other ideas is important to resolving anger. Also, ask God to find a new way.

> Larry, an older student at Teen Challenge, was trying to use the toaster for his breakfast. While the bread was toasting, he went to get the rest of his breakfast. When he returned, he found that someone had removed his bread from the toaster and put in two English muffins. After checking around, he found out that Peter was the culprit. There had been a developing history of quiet agitation between the

two for weeks. Consequently, when this situation occurred, the stored up anger inside Larry burst forth with aggressive anger.

Larry brought the incident to my *Anger Reconciliation* class where he tried unsuccessfully to practice RAA on Peter about the incident. Peter, a new 17-year-old student, acted very defensively and would not acknowledge his role. In desperation, Larry asked Randy, an older student in the program, to help him. Randy became a mediator for both of them in the pattern given in Mathew 18:16 (see the beginning of the next chapter for details). Using his experience, Randy was able to have both of them talk about their real feelings about each other. Then, he developed a plan how both of them could talk to each other about their irritations. Also, he emphasized sharing with each other. These creative ideas worked and Larry and Peter had no more incidents.

Thanking God for his help. When we are finished using RAA, we need to thank God for His help in resolving or trying to resolve the situation. God needs to get the glory for any steps that are achieved. That way we don't get prideful. Even if the situation if not resolved to our satisfaction, God is working in all parties. Thus we ask the other person to pray, thanking God for His help. If the other person, doesn't want to or is not a Christian, you need to pray separately.

The last A of RAA is for anger. Therefore, we have a new and positive way to express our anger, RAA. I have found it to be very successful in resolving situations not only when I am angry, but when people are angry at me. However, I must utilize all the principles and steps of RAA as best as I can to achieve success. Prayer to God is critical to RAA's success; without it RAA will not work, or only have limited success.

The equation for RAA is:

Threat → Anxiety → Using RAA → Reconciliation for all parties

Evaluating RAA in the following categories:

Respect for others—very high for everyone involved. Respect is the key to RAA's success. It reflects God's critical guidance to the process.

Relationships—enhanced by the care shown to all parties in the RAA process. In fact, deep relationships require going through an anger situation successfully.

Control—God-directed process, which creates success. Everyone participates actively with a sense of freedom.

Frustrations—limited as long as one is patient. It will take time for the RAA process to work and this should be understood upfront.

Emotional maturity—very high since people are asked to grow emotionally. They are able to develop a greater sensitivity to others and God.

Long-term effect—RAA provides the most useful form of positive anger that we all need for many of our everyday anger issues. I have personally used it successfully for almost 12 years. Those who have tried RAA give testimony to its success over this time period. Using RAA instead of negative anger leads to reconciliation or harmony for everyone involved. What a blessing!

> Charlie, a student at Syracuse Teen Challenge had attended my "Anger Reconciliation" classes for over three months. He had listened carefully and had participated in the practice exercises that we did. Charlie developed an easy grasp of the RAA process from practicing it. Then one day he was put to the test with a real angry situation. A new student started disrespecting him verbally. His old way would have

been to use aggressive anger on the other student. This time, however, he tried RAA and with God's help, it worked. The disrespect stopped. He kept lauding how RAA worked so well.

I hope that by now the reader is motivated enough to want to seriously consider dropping negative anger and try using RAA in his/her own anger situations. RAA with the biblical principles, needs to be tried several times to be successful. With God's help, you also will find success and want to adopt RAA as your main anger expression. A prayer for my anger expression might be:

Lord, how can I start expressing my anger in a life-giving way?

From reviewing the three positive anger expressions we see that anger, expressed in a positive way, can produce positive results. This should help us to treat the word anger differently by distinguishing between positive and negative anger expressions. This is one of my goals in writing this book.

We all have the option to choose our own anger expression. In Chapter Two, we have seen the pain caused by the three negative anger expressions. After reading Chapter Three, you have now become aware of three better options of expressing our anger. Hopefully, you see the benefits of harmony by using positive anger, especially RAA. It is my hope that you will want to start using one or more of the positive anger expressions. I realize that there may be obstacles to changing our anger expression to RAA, which we shall address in the next chapter.

Summary:

1. Seek reconciliation or peace for all parties when resolving our anger.

2. Use God to help us resolve our anger through prayer.

3. Biblical principles to use for resolving anger positively: respect, acknowledging the freedom of others to make their own choices,

being optimistic, establishing a dialogue with the other person, emotional maturity, patience and seeking the truth.

4. Types of positive anger: Righteous Anger, Releasing Anger and Respective Assertive Anger.

5. Righteous Anger—when we stand up for our values especially Christian values.

6. Releasing Anger includes: dropping anger and forgiveness of anger.

7. Respectful Assertive Anger (RAA)—the steps for Respectful are: praying for peace, to use the right words in the right way, and for the other person to receive our words. Then approach the person in a friendly manner, sit down next to the person and ask the person to pray together.

Assertiveness includes: caring for the other's feelings, staying calm and persistent, listening to what they are saying, focusing my eyes on the other person to see their body language, keeping my hands visible, being brief and clear when talking, seeking the truth, setting a boundary and being creative with new ideas to resolve the problem.

Discussion Questions

1. Have you ever used righteous anger in your life? What were the results?

2. Do you have any anxieties about using righteous anger? Explain.

3. Explain dropping anger. Is it an anger expression that you could use?

4. Explain RAA in your own terms.

5. Do you think RAA could help you with your anger? If not, why not?

Chapter 4
Challenges to Using RAA

After learning about RAA and positive anger expressions, you may want to change your anger expression to one of them. You may, however, feel stopped by one or more of the following:

My emotions overwhelm me. When I get angry my emotions take control and I can only express my anger in a negative way. Does that sound like you? Thus, RAA sounds like a good option for my anger, but how do I control my emotions enough to use it? Some people have confirmed to me that they are unable to use RAA because they get too emotional. The question is, do I trust God more than my emotions? When I get angry, before I encounter the other person, can I commit to praying for peace for my emotions? In a sense, we can make feelings an idol when we trust them more than God. Dr. Les Carter in, *The Anger Trap,* shows how our emotions can trap (control) our lives: "People who are trapped by their own anger tend to let their emotional direction be determined by instinct or reflex reaction to an undesirable circumstance. Little thought may be given to the purpose of the emotion." As a result, we do not think about the consequences of being controlled by our emotions. As Christians, we want to be directed by God to think and act in a godly way. Can I trust God to let Him take control of my emotions?

Suggested Solution: Pray to God daily to have Him help you with your emotions when angry. When angry, commit to praying for emotional peace BEFORE talking to the other person. Ask God to help you use RAA for your anger expression.

Sandra, a Christian woman for 30 years, loved the Lord and prayed to Him daily. She had a tender caring personality that wanted to help others just like the Bible tells us. She felt empathy for others with such passion that often she would cry for their difficult situations. However, when angry, this compassionate person would explode with aggressive anger just like her father. She would say, "I have to get it (my anger) out." This led to painful results and she wanted to change this negative anger pattern. Nevertheless, she felt controlled by her emotions. "If only I could get control of my emotions when I get angry," she would say. Finally, with much prayer and introspection with God's direction, she gained control of her emotions. As a result, she felt more emotional peace.

A bondage of lies controls my anger expression. If we let lies control us, they can prevent us from being able to change our anger expression. I have personally seen this bondage occurring in Christian people. I have seen their lies exposed and healed by Jesus by using Theophastic Prayer Ministry (TPM). This process involves a leader guiding a person with questions revealing the emotions of a painful memory, then bringing these feelings to Jesus in prayer for truth and peace. Thus, Jesus does the real healing. It is from our feelings that our beliefs are formed. These beliefs may or may not be true. Many times we harbor lies from the past that control our emotions and actions. When Jesus heals us of our lies, we feel a new peace in our lives and a new sense of freedom.

I belong to a group that meets twice per month to learn and practice TPM. There we learn how to use TPM correctly from watching videos showing the founder of TPM, Ed Smith, modeling this counseling technique. During one of these meetings, I experienced a personal revelation when TPM was practiced on me. I asked for prayer about my experience with my father just before he died. My father had called me from a Florida nursing home where he had gone the day before. He told me that he wasn't sure how long he would live. In my concern, I flew down and immediately went to the nursing home to see him. There I saw him looking frailer than I had ever seen him. He was 81 years old, but was able to talk.

I arrived there about 11:00 AM and stayed till 9:30 PM closing. We used that time talking about our family and I asked him about being saved. He had not accepted Jesus in his heart and life, while I had done so six months earlier. I talked to my dad about what would happen to him after his death. He answered me with, "I have my own private faith," which he wouldn't explain despite my asking him several times. As a new born-again Christian, I had zeal to bring my father to Christ, particularly given his circumstances. He continued to resist me throughout the day. I asked God for strength, but my father was immoveable. I prayed with him before I left, but felt great frustration and later I asked God to take him. He died the next morning before I could see him again causing me great guilt. This pain brought me to the TPM meeting for prayer. The pastor's wife used TPM on me and Jesus released me from my guilt feelings of that night giving me a feeling of peace—Praise God!

If you are unaware of TPM, they have a website www.theophostic.com. Additionally the founder, Ed Smith has written several books about it. I have used it successfully on some of the students that I have mentored at Syracuse Teen Challenge.

Being comfortable with our own anger expression even if it is negative. Many people develop a comfort level with their own anger because they think they are getting the results THEY want. They may see secondary gains from their negative anger like controlling others or getting their way. As a result, they feel comfortable with their negative anger expression, which becomes a habit that is very difficult to break. We oftentimes don't realize how the receiver of that negative anger feels. Is there resentment? If so, there will eventually be a counter reaction of some type, including avoiding us. Do you want people to avoid you because of your anger expression? You probably wouldn't continue with your present anger expression if you realized its effect on others. Feeling lonely or rejected by others can be a painful feeling.

Suggested Solution: You explore the other person's reactions and feelings to your anger expression before you continue with negative anger. Then try RAA several times and discuss the results with the other person. You will probably notice a greater measure of peace in your life.

> Janet, a born-again Christian, developed a method of sarcasm to express her anger. It seemed very effective in getting her point across with a special zing to it. She felt a sense of exhilaration with her sarcasm. Feeling the sting of that sarcasm, however, people would stay away from her. Over the years, the sharpness of her sarcasm became stronger. Finally, during a strong argument, her oldest daughter confronted her with how painful it felt. Shocked at how great an effect it had on her daughter, Janet changed and dropped the sarcasm.

Our anger triggers control our anger. These triggers from Chapter One are:

Family or generational patterns. These anger patterns are taught (modeled) to us as children including the form of anger expression.

Accordingly, aggressive fathers model aggressive anger to their children. This anger pattern can also include little things that provoke anger in our parents like cleanliness, or driving habits. We learn these in childhood and pass them on to later generations, if they are not stopped. Unfortunately, the patterns we saw expressed as children oftentimes are repeated by us on our children. Later our children repeat this same anger pattern so that it continues for generations. These triggers are very strongly embedded in our psyche and therefore difficult to change.

Suggested Solution: Pray for God to remove this generational sin from us. Because of the ingrown nature of generational anger, it is difficult to change and requires great persistence to correct. Sometimes Christian counseling is necessary to remove this negative past before change is possible.

> As a teenager, my father would ask me to drive the family car when we took short trips. He wanted to control my driving by constantly correcting me to fit his driving style. I was not a bad driver. His constant correction, however, grated on my nerves, causing me to feel anger. Several times, I told him that he was making me angry with his constant corrections. Then I told him to either be quiet or do the driving himself. Later, when teaching my son how to drive, I found myself wanting to do the very same thing that I had hated. It was instinctual (generational). The same desire for control came out in me. Fortunately, I realized what I was about to do and stopped. At times, I found I even had to cover my mouth to prevent myself from saying something controlling. With God's help my need for control went away.

Our personality. Some personalities gravitate towards different types of anger. As stated in Chapter One, aggressive people usually use aggressive anger and quiet people use stuffing or passive-aggressive anger. We each feel a comfort with our own type of anger expression. It seems to fit well with who we are. As we know from Chapter Two aggressive anger produces more anger, not resolution. Also, we may be impatient people. This conflicts with the RAA process which requires patience. As a result, RAA may seem beyond our apparent abilities. As Christians, however, we are asked to grow in the Holy Spirit. The development of patience is a mark of Christian maturity that we need to develop.

Suggested Solution: Come to God to help us grow more Christ-like with our personality. He can modify our uncaring characteristics to better reflect Jesus.

> Tina was an impatient person and her anger reflect-ed that. Her impatience, accompanied with critical anger, flowed out to everyone around her. This anger created great stress for everyone, including Tina, and then she would become even more angry. When asked to modify her behavior, she would say, "That's just the way I am. Take it, or leave it." That uncaring attitude caused people to go out of their way to avoid her. Unfortunately, she still has not changed and continues to suffer from critical anger.

Our experience. As we grow up, we usually explore different options including different anger expressions. This situation can be particular-ly true when our negative anger continues to result in our feeling hurt and/or frustrated. Usually, we only know about the three negative forms of anger, so our pain and frustration continues.

Suggested Solution: With our new knowledge of positive anger expressions, especially RAA, we need to explore using it. Because of the pain of our negative results, we should want to try a new positive anger expression.

Poor communication abilities. Some people are not able to express themselves comfortably. They lack the skills of listening well and/or expressing their anger. They get frustrated easily when placed in a situation requiring them to express themselves clearly. This inability is particularly true of some men. Because of their weak communication abilities, they will not even try to use RAA. I have noticed at Teen Challenge that once a poor communicator sees others successfully practicing RAA they will usually at least try it. The key is asking God to help us overcome the fear, or our inability to communicate.

Suggested Solution: Go through the steps of RAA on your own by asking God to help you overcome your communication limitations. Also, you can practice RAA several times with a friend or spouse so that both of you can learn it and overcome your inabilities.

> Tommy, an eighteen-year-old student at Teen Challenge, had great energy and aggressive anger. He also had some learning difficulties, which made it hard for him to express himself. He attended my "Anger Reconciliation" class four times. During that time, I specifically did not call on him to practice RAA. However, he was able to see others successfully practice RAA and to see where they failed. (In our sessions, we have volunteers who agree to role play using RAA in an angry situation). Gradually, I could see that he was becoming more comfortable with RAA as he participated in the discussions. Then, I asked him to practice RAA. At first he was reluctant, but with encouragement, he tried it. Tommy, with God's help, did fairly well. After class, he was so excited and grateful that he had tried. He asked me if he could have the opportunity to practice RAA again. You could see his confidence had received a big boost.

This example was not an isolated incident. I have had similar successful experiences with other students at Teen Challenge over 12 years. It can be true for you as well, as long as you try with God's help.

Lack of perseverance. Sometimes we fail at RAA the first time and get discouraged. This feeling can result in our not trying again. Perseverance means patient endurance of hardship or overcoming discouragement. Accordingly, when we fail in our attempt at trying RAA, God wants us to persevere. James 1:1-4 (NIV) says, *"Consider it pure joy, my brothers, because you know that the testing of your faith develops perseverance. Perseverance must finish its work so that you may be mature and complete, lacking nothing."* Thus, when we fail to try RAA, James encourages us to persevere by trying again and again. Through our attempts, we are gaining maturity, which is one of our goals in this life. By using perseverance, we will have a greater chance to succeed with RAA.

    Suggested Solution: Perseverance means not giving up, especially when we fail when using RAA. By seeking God's help to become more persistent in using RAA, we will succeed. I have seen it done many times at Teen Challenge.

> Michael said, "I've tried this RAA thing and it just doesn't work for me. I'm going back to my old anger!" I talked to him about his old anger style of passive-aggressive anger and the negative results it produced. We talked and he finally agreed that the results were not always the best. Still, he didn't want to try RAA again. He seemed frustrated with the lack of positive results with RAA. We read the above verses and talked about being persistent. I asked him to pray for God's help and then try RAA again. He did and one week later and he told me he had some success. This event proved to be a growth point for him in his Christian walk and he is now using RAA regularly.

Self-defeating behaviors. These include several different poor choices that you and I make over time. These choices negatively affect our lives including our anger expressions. These are:

Use of drugs or alcohol. They can prevent us from being able to use RAA because our minds are clouded. Our speech and actions are negatively affected and thus we are unable to use RAA in angry situations. The drugs are oftentimes used to medicate our pain or inadequacies. They don't solve our problems and, in fact, delay solving them. As I have seen at Teen Challenge, men have delayed their spiritual and emotional growth by using drugs. It does give a temporary relief, but that relief is illusionary. By not really dealing with our issues, we stay like children. We make drugs an idol and don't trust God to help us with our problems.

Suggested Solution: Commit to trusting in God's help versus trusting in drugs. Seek help through successful Christian drug treatment programs like Teen Challenge.

> Eduardo was from Brooklyn, NY. He started taking drugs at 13 and by 21 had become a full-time addict. By 25, he was sick and tired of the drug scene. Seeking to change, he sought out Teen Challenge. Once in the program, he felt the lure back to drugs just to calm down. While in the program, he found a way to get a small pack of cigarettes, which he smoked occasionally. He was unwilling to practice RAA in my class. Also, he developed a bad attitude, which tested all the staff. Then, we discovered the cigarettes. After being expelled, he went back to drugs, but found it worse this time. He called and came back with new resolve to overcome the drugs in his life. He also participated actively in my class and successfully used RAA. With God's help, he was a changed man and drug free and resolved his anger issue.

A decline in spiritual life. This happens when we deny the priority of God in our lives. The decline in spiritual life works against RAA being used, since dependency on God is a focal point of RAA. If we give Satan control of our lives, he wants to work against RAA by encouraging negative anger between people. Therefore, it is imperative for us to counter Satan with God's help. If I find that my relationship with God is weakening, I need to recognize this and do things that will strengthen that relationship.

Suggested Solution: Try worshipping God daily in our lives and also going regularly to church. Praying is our real means of communication with God so we need to start there. Then, reading the Bible is important. These actions will help us to rebuild that critical relationship with Christ. He will give us new confidence to make RAA work.

Decline in moral values. This occurs when we seek worldly values to the detriment of Godly values. To achieve our selfish goals, we manipulate our lives by lying, cheating, etc. Decline in moral values will many times result in our lying to get what we want. In effect, we live in bondage to the lies in our lives. Decline in moral values negatively affects our self-image and causes us to act out of fear and doubt. The focus of RAA is also finding the truth, while negative anger thrives on lies to obscure the truth.

Suggested Solution: Come to God to give you the strength to follow godly morals. You will find a new freedom and confidence by following Christian morality. Then, you can use RAA in your anger situations.

> Andy came to Teen Challenge with habits of lying, swearing and seeking his own way. While he had grown up without a father who left when Andy was four, his mother was a Christian woman. Unfortunately, her faith was not adopted by her son, who was drawn by worldly friends with wrong values. This decision caused him to lack a moral compass in his life. He started using drugs at 13. He was now 22

with a good mind, but was unable to use it in a positive way. Unfortunately, he used his wits to sell drugs for a living. His drug habit brought him to Teen Challenge. These wrong moral values caused him to have problems adapting to the Teen Challenge program. Andy was unable to practice RAA well because of these old values, particularly lying. As he developed a personal relationship with Jesus, the lying stopped and his moral values changed. Then, using the truth, he was able to use RAA effectively.

Fear of change. A profound alarm is set off in us when we perceive danger coming from changes in our lives. This alarm may be real, or imagined. This fear is usually developed in infancy. We don't like the anxiety feeling that change brings because of the uncertainty of its outcome. Usually people who fear change tend to seek safety in the way they construct their lives. They develop strong habits and resist the growth that change can bring them. As a result, changing their anger expression to RAA can represent a major challenge. They can see it practiced and still not want to change from their negative anger expression(s). God does not want us to live in fear as stated in Isaiah 41:10 (NIV): *"So do not fear, for I am with you; do not be dismayed, for I am your God. I will strengthen you and help you; I will uphold you with my righteous hand."* The verse tells us if we depend on God for His strength and not our own, then we will not live in fear.

Suggested Solution: Trust in God's wisdom for His solution rather than your own wisdom for a solution. God's strength will break the bonds of fear in our lives. With God's help and exposure over time to RAA's successes, we can overcome our fear of change.

Inability to develop dialogue. Dialogue is a process of feedback and mutual understanding. It is more than a casual conversation; it is a progressive sharing of our inner selves and feelings with others. Some people lack the skills to develop dialogue. This inability starts in childhood where these skills are developed. Also, a person's inhibited personality may result in a lack of skill in being able to dialogue. Such a limitation, however, does not commit them to a life without dialogue. Through perseverance, studying and practicing successful ways, these early problems can be overcome.

> I was one of those people who was shy growing up, complicated by a learning disability—dyslexia. This combination made it difficult for me to dialogue with people as a youngster. However, my mother always encouraged me to persist to overcome my problems. She told me to never give up, which I still remember and practice to this day. With my mother's daily practices with me and God's blessing, I was gradually able to overcome the dyslexia after several years. I learned from observing others how to make dialogue successful, which developed new confidence in my abilities.

Good communication and listening skills are necessary for dialogue to be effective. To achieve this ability takes practice and persistence. Our angry situations may not create friends, but they can provide an opportunity to turn a difficult, or even a painful situation, into a better relationship. I have found that even with apparent enemies, dialogue can develop with respect and understanding, while not having mutual agreement.

Suggested Solution: I am indebted to the book, *Design for Wellness,* and its chapter on dialogue for providing some of the following concepts on dialogue:

Develop listening skills. Try reflective listening as described in Chapter Three—repeating back, as exactly as possible, what the other person has said. Reflective listening requires us to listen closely and remember what was said. I need to listen well to be able to understand what the other person is saying. Listening also requires us to hear the emotions of the other person as words and emotions may differ. In such a case the emotions usually tell the true story. Body language can reveal true emotions such as not looking you in the eyes, face down, crossed arms and legs and back turned to you. Listening does not mean arguing. Also, listening requires us to hear what is not said. This may mean asking the person to repeat what they said so you can grasp it. I have found that sometimes when a person is really hurting about something, they may be afraid to reveal it. Is there another message being sent? With attention and practice, listening well will come.

Proverbs 18:13 points out the importance of listening: *"He who answers before listening—that is his folly and his shame."* If we learn to listen first, our speech will be wiser and more measured so that we will be responding and not reacting, which is often the case. Thus we will be slower to anger and in fact our angry situations will be reduced.

Clarity and completeness. I have found that my misunderstandings leading to arguments arise because of lack of clearly saying what I want or mean. Too often I hear vague comments like, "I want you to act responsible," without detailing exactly what area we want or how we want them to be responsible. This lack of specifics will lead to differences in expectations and, therefore, future arguments. I have found it is important to take the time to spell out what you want and ask if there are any questions. When someone is vague it is important to stop them and ask them to be specific. Even if they have explained what they want, you may not agree as they are setting up something they expect from you. When in doubt it is better to over explain rather than under explain your requests.

Understanding the message being sent. To truly understand means to connect with the message the other person is sending. Understanding the message involves receiving the ideas and feelings of others without trying to fix the person. Women particularly want men to listen and empathize with them in their situation. Thus, women don't want us as men to necessarily fix the problem. Men, on the other hand, may seek advice from another man, which when given, will be greatly appreciated. Consequently, understanding comes with a desire to show love for that person through our kindness and interest in them. We need to do our best to grasp the other person's needs and relate to them with godly kindness.

> Gina loved her husband, Neal, and they had been happily married for over 25 years. They were Christians who loved the Lord and read the Bible almost daily. Yet, when Gina got disturbed over her fears of rejection from others and she wanted to discuss it with Neal, he couldn't listen to her. Her fears triggered fear in him so that he just wanted to end the discussion by "fixing" her problem. Accordingly, Gina became frustrated. She would say: "Just listen to me; don't try to fix it!" Neal, seeing her frustration and wanting to love her, tried his best to listen to her. Gradually, with God's help and with greater patience, he was better able to truly listen and reflect her feelings. These actions helped their relationship, but he still struggles at times to listen and understand her as well as she would like. Understanding is a continuous progression of learning how to better connect with the other person.

Don't judge the other person. This usually causes us to put the person down. The Bible calls us to confront wrong actions but not judge the person. Only God is able to do that successfully. Consequently, judging a person will break dialogue and even the relationship. Also, we need to try to understand differences in the other people, which enriches our lives. Even if they seem ungodly, as Christians we can try to understand and show kindness to others even when we don't agree. However, we are not to compromise on our fundamental Christian values. As stated previously, we can agree to disagree.

Willing to share our inner selves with others is to risk being vulnerable with others about our deepest feelings and hurts. Sharing ourselves does not happen immediately, but reflects a confidence in ourselves. This opening up reveals our real self and provides an opportunity for deeper dialogue.

Having an open mind to accept change means my willingness to accept change in my life, provided the godly evidence supports such a change. I find that some people want me to change my life without respecting my right to have a different plan. First, I want to seek God's direction before making any changes in my life. Once He confirms that such a change is part of His plans, He will give me the tools to effectuate such a change.

Hopefully, we can put these above steps into action to enable us to establish dialogue for our angry situations.

We have seen a number of the real challenges to using RAA to express our anger. These represent a lack of emotional and spiritual growth in our lives. God wants us to grow and become mature and using RAA represents that opportunity for us.

My prayer continual prayer is: *Oh God, help us to overcome these impediments to using RAA and help us to use it for expressing our anger!*

Summary:

1. Reasons why I don't use RAA: My anger emotions overwhelm me. I'm comfortable with my current anger expression.

Anger triggers control me. They include: family background, personality and experiences. Other reasons include:
Poor communication ability
Lack of perseverance
Self-defeating behaviors
Fear of change
Inability to develop dialogue

2. Self-defeating behaviors are: use of drugs or alcohol, decline in spiritual life and decline in moral values.

3. Steps to develop dialogue: Develop listening skills
Understanding the message sent
Don't judge others
Willing to share our inner selves
Having an open mind to accept change

Discussion Questions

1. What issues are holding you back from using RAA for your anger expression?

2. If you have self-defeating problems, can you get help to overcome them?

3. Do you have any other issues, not listed above, with using RAA? If so, what are they? Can you see a way to overcome them?

4. Do you find that your lack of communication skills inhibit you from using RAA? How can these be overcome?

Chapter 5

Other Important Concepts that Ensure Success

Over the 15 years of teaching about anger at Teen Challenge and diverse groups at churches I thank God to have identified several very useful factors to help us express our anger in a better way. I have found that these factors are important because they can make a significant difference between success and failure in expressing our anger positively.

Using Matthew 18:15-17 for disputes between Christians. Jesus tells here how to resolve our anger between brothers and sisters in Christ: *"If your brother sins against you, go and show him his fault, just between the two of you. If he listens to you, you have won your brother over. But if he will not listen, take one or two others along, so that every matter may be established by the testimony of two or three witnesses. If he refuses to listen to them, tell it to the church and if he refuses to listen to the church, treat him as you would a pagan or a tax collector."*

It is important to realize that this process is only for use between Christians (non-Christians won't understand what you are doing). Also, Matthew 18:15-17 is for dealing only with sins directed towards us and not towards others. We require the students at Syracuse Teen Challenge to use this process when someone (either students or staff) offends them personally. It is not applicable if the offense involves breaking the rules of Teen Challenge.

A breakdown of the verses shows:

18:15 *"If your brother sins against you, go and show him his fault, just between the two of you. If he listens to you, you have won your brother over."* It is an attempt to resolve the issue on a one-to-one basis and shows respect for the other person. Also, it avoids the usual forms of negative anger expression such as revenge or gossip. With God's help, the anger issue can be resolved peacefully and without others getting involved. Using RAA to resolve the situation is strongly recommended because it involves God and shows respect for all parties. It is critical, however, that the offending person listen and respond correctly. He or she needs to apologize, or at least recognize, that what they did was wrong. We usually ask the Teen Challenge students to ask the offending student to confirm that he will not commit the same offense again. The offending person's words and, most importantly, his subsequent actions, will reflect whether he is serious about changing. If both words and actions of the offending person change, then you have won your brother (sister) over. Then, the offended person should forgive the other person so that no bitterness takes root. What we seek is the truth of the situation. Truth is important since Satan tries to create angry situations with lies. We need to be aware of this tactic and seek God's truth.

If the person in error apologizes, but continues to walk (his actions continue) in the SAME sinful way, he has not acknowledged his offense. In effect, the offending person may be manipulating the situation for his own self-interest or have a hardened heart. Then, the offended person MUST go on to 18:16. I have found that one of the major problems with implementing Matthew 18:15-17 is that Teen Challenge students continue to use only 18:15 for the same issue. This action defeats the purpose of the escalating consequences of the verses and has proven unproductive to resolving angry situations. Note if the offending person commits a DIFFERENT sin, then you must start again with 18:15 for that sin.

> Ryan was angry with Ted for constantly taking his pen during "Personal Studies" class at Teen Challenge. Ryan had asked Ted not to take his pen anymore, but Ted said he was only playing around. Therefore, Ryan brought this situation to my "Anger Reconciliation" class to work it out. He carefronted

Ted using the RAA principles and told Ted to stop taking his pen. Ryan explained how it was not funny when Ted took the pen. Ted realized that he needed to stop and he agreed to do so. He also apologized to Ryan for starting the foolishness. Both students were pleased with the result.

(Note while Matthew 18:15 states to do this in private, practicing it in the class helped all the members to learn how to use Matthew 18:15-17. We practice this in every class with different students to help them see the positive effects of RAA and Matthew 18:15-17).

18:16 *"But if he will not listen, take one or two others along, so that every matter may be established by the testimony of two or three witnesses."* This principle is implemented when the offending person refuses to correct his behavior. Therefore, more people now need to be involved. The Scriptures say two or three witnesses. Again, the verse reflects the desire to give respect by limiting the number of people involved. The goal is also to resolve the situation peacefully, seeking the truth.

The witnesses are there to perform two functions: to testify to the truth of what was said and done plus act as mediators to help resolve the situation. From my classes at Teen Challenge, I have found that witnesses can be very instrumental in resolving conflicts with creative solutions. As a result, it is important to select quality neutral witnesses. The offended party should select the witnesses. They should not be friends of either party in the dispute and ideally they should have some experience with being a witness in these situations. The witnesses' goal is not to take sides, but to find the truth and a workable solution for both parties.

Darrell had become angry with Jesse over an incident in the dorm room. Apparently Jesse had put shaving cream on Darrell's bed during the early evening.

When Darrell went to bed later, he got all messed up from the shaving cream. He checked around and discovered that Jesse was the guilty party. Darrell told Jesse that he was angry with what he had done. By circumstance, I was having my class that night so Darrell brought up the situation. Jesse, however, denied it and kept claiming that he wasn't the one.

Following Matthew 18:16 principles, Darrell selected Van and Leonard to be witnesses. They met with Jesse who continued his denial. Then Van explained how he had seen him with a shaving cream container in his hands at the time of the incident. With the truth revealed, Jesse reluctantly admitted his actions and apologized.

Matthew 18:17 This verse says, *"If he refuses to listen to them, tell it to the church and if he refuses to listen even to the church, treat him as you would a pagan or a tax collector."* Jesus is telling us to keep the process of resolving the situation in the church rather than taking it to the outside community. In the church, God is there to help develop a solution. The goal is correcting a brother (sister) who has done wrong and implementing a plan of restoration. This process is to be done with respect and concern. For those Christians not in Teen Challenge, we should take the issue to our churches for resolution, using the pastor and/or the church board.

At Syracuse Teen Challenge, this means taking the issue to a general meeting with the students. That is our "church." There, the leaders question the participants including the witnesses, to determine the truth as best as possible. The leaders prayerfully seek God's direction and His correction.

Frank had become very angry at Grant who was constantly attacking him with verbal barbs. Using these Matthew 18:15-17 principles, Frank had brought this to Grant's attention using 18:15 without success. He later went to 18:16 and Grant denied that he was doing this. Grant claimed it was Frank's fault for always bringing it up. Finally, Frank brought the situation to our meeting where Grant continued to deny the problem. After questioning the two parties, the Teen Challenge leaders decided to have them pray together for a while. Also, Grant was required to examine himself for denial using several Scriptures that we gave him. This combination seemed to have worked and the barbs stopped.

Reversal is a defensive measure used by a person who is being confronted. This person feels vulnerable to correction so he goes on the offensive by pointing out problems in the other person. This vulnerability often times is a symptom of pride. In *The Anger Workbook* by Dr. Les Carter and Dr. Frank Minirith they explain reversal in this way: "When we use reversal techniques we assume others are out to get us, so we become offensive whenever delicate matters are discussed." There is no progress made in resolving the anger issue brought up with this type of defensiveness. The person has fear of admitting a weakness, which is an important part of resolution. Note: reversal can be especially a problem with men.

Suggested solution: When someone tries this tactic, tell them that they are trying to use reversal. Let them know that they can bring up their problem later after resolving the first anger issue. Otherwise, nothing will be accomplished as the two parties argue back and forth. This is Satan's way of keeping discord alive.

Tim was tall and thin and in his 40s when he came into Teen Challenge. He was intelligent and very articulate. He also appeared to do well in his classes. Unfortunately, he could not accept correction. Thus, when he was "carefronted" in my class, he would always

use reversal on the other person. The situation got so
bad that we finally called him "Mr. Reversal." This
inability to accept godly correction led to his down-
fall and his pride kept him drug dependent for years.

The use of time out. This is a successful technique that God revealed
to me as a way to help reduce the emotions of the other person at a
time of conflict. Some people let their emotions take over when they
get angry and try to dominate the other person with aggressive anger.
This action can result in the emotional person being unable to listen
or receive what the other person is saying. Sometimes the other person may use reversal as well. I discovered from God that using a time
out for prayer would break that emotional control. Even if the other
person didn't want to pray, I found that I still needed to pray. If the
prayer didn't work the first time, I needed to persist in praying until
the other person's emotions calmed down. Then, real dialogue and
mutual understanding could occur. My experience has shown that
time out does work with God's help.

> Karen was upset with a problem of disrespect she
> had with another employee at work. She came home
> disturbed in her spirit and started discussing this
> with her husband, Herb. She started talking in a loud
> agitated voice. She wanted to keep talking without
> giving Herb a chance to comment. Every time he
> started to talk, she would interrupt him, which
> became frustrating to Herb. He could see that she
> was so controlled by her emotions that he couldn't
> dialogue with her. He remembered about the "time
> out" concept, so he invited her to pray. She flatly
> refused his offer. Therefore, he prayed by himself for
> God to bring some peace to the situation. Again, he
> tried talking, but Karen was still so emotionally upset
> she wouldn't listen. Consequently, he prayed again

with the same results. Finally, the third time it worked as there was more calm and they could dialogue and get some peace for her anger.

Staying away from close association with constantly angry people. Avoid close association with constantly angry people that will tend to affect us with their negative anger. Through our close association with the constant anger, our expression of anger will gradually become negative, if we are not careful. The Scripture in Proverbs 22:24-25 addresses this issue: *"Do not make friends with a hot-tempered man, do not associate with one easily angered or you may learn his ways, and get yourself ensnared."* Accordingly, this hot-tempered anger is contagious and should be avoided. As Chuck Swindoll states in his book *Man to Man:* "Are you becoming an angry person because you're associating closely with angry people? The Scripture says, 'Don't do it!'" Accordingly, we need to watch our associations as they may seriously affect our anger expression.

> Ernie came to Teen Challenge as an angry 31-year-old man. His childhood had been tough growing up with a single mother as his father had left the house when he was six. Later, he drifted into street gangs and selling drugs. After getting caught for robbery for the third time, he spent eight years in jail, which truly hardened him. His anger seemed to rise up quickly whenever he was asked to submit to a rule, or an authority figure. He didn't want friends and liked being a loner. The other students responded by staying away except one student, Lou, who seemed to be drawn to him. They had like backgrounds and gradually they become friends. In time, the anger that Lou expressed was just like Ernie's. They were like twins with their anger. Finally, Ernie left the program and Lou's anger expression gradually moderated.

Avoid smiling or laughing when expressing anger. When expressing our anger, any smiling or laughter seriously distracts from the valid message we are sending. Laughter may be the result of nervousness that a person feels when in an angry situation. But it still distracts from the serious intent of the message and should be avoided at all costs. The smiling can also cause the receiver to wonder, "Is this person really serious about what they are saying?" Consequently, laughing and/or smiling presents a confusing message to the person receiving the message. Is that what you want?

Suggested solution: If you find that you are nervous about "carefronting" someone with positive anger, pray to God for help with your laughter before approaching them. Also, if someone is smiling at you in an angry situation, ask them if they are serious about what they are saying. These actions usually cause the person smiling or laughing to become serious and stop smiling.

> Felix was a 17-year-old student who came from Long Island to Syracuse Teen Challenge for help. His Christian parents were at their wit's end with his disruptive behavior. He had an easy smile, which often developed into laughter when confronted with an angry situation. When his laughter was discussed in my "Anger Reconciliation Class" he explained how angry situations made him nervous when having to carefront others. After discussing the distractions that laughter and smiling cause in resolving anger, he knew that he needed to change. He prayed to be serious in angry situations and, in time, the smiling went away. As a result, he became more effective with his expression of anger.

Talking out our anger with a counselor or friend. Being able to talk out our feelings of anger with a trusted person can help release those angry feelings. This discussion is particularly helpful when we are confused by an angry situation and some neutral but caring person can give us a new perspective. Sometimes our immediate feelings can mislead us into feeling negative anger when, in reality, we are controlled by Satan. That is why we need help. We recommend going to God with the problem, but another person can be God's representative for us. A good Christian friend, who is able to deal with their anger in a godly way, can be very helpful in working through painful feelings of anger. In *The Anger Workbook* the authors amplify the value of discussing your anger with a trusted friend: "When you confess your anger to a trusted friend, two things can occur: 1) You are able to find help and support from someone who loves you, and 2) you feel more accountable to follow through with your plans to be emotionally appropriate in the future." Then, you will deal with the person you are angry with in a godly way. Your chances for a positive resolution are much better.

> Jean, a women in her 40s, had an aggressive anger that would come out quickly. Over the years this resulted in her losing relationships, which was very painful for her. The negative modeling from her mother's aggressive anger seemed to have established this negative pattern in Jean's life forever. The pain of these experiences, however, caused her to seek help from her friend, Pat. From her own Christian counseling experience, Pat suggested that Jean call Pat whenever she got angry. These calls proved to be very helpful as they allowed Jean to reduce her emotions and deal with the problem in a godly way. Gradually, Jean learned a new way of dealing with her anger and the calls stopped.

The distance factor. This is the physical distance we need to keep between ourselves and others when meeting them so they don't get irritated. This distance will vary between people, but if a person is right on top of someone else, they will become angry, or at least nervous.

Being aware of this is important in angry situations as violating some-one's space can create more anger. The importance of the distance fac-tor was brought to my attention by students in my class at Syracuse Teen Challenge.

Suggested solution: When I'm talking to someone, I need to be aware of how close I am to them. If I don't know them, I need to give them enough distance between us. If they seem nervous, I may need to create more distance between us and watch their body language for signs of anxiety. As I get to know someone better, they will "invite me" to come closer or they may want a distant relationship. Be sensitive to what distance makes a person comfortable.

> With another friend, I have taught a Bible study in the men's shelter of the Syracuse Rescue Mission for 19 years. In my first year, I was going around to the men asking them if they would come to our Bible study. One day, I approached a tall thin man who looked intensely at me as I started talking. He got up and started to walk towards me with his fists clenched. I started backing up and prayed to God for help. Raising my hands in a surrender-like position, I kept walking backward while praying to God. Suddenly he stopped and went back to his seat. The supervisor at the shelter told me I had violated his space, which set off his anger. That lesson has stayed with me when meeting new people.

Creating an emotional word picture to better express anger. Emotional word pictures is a concept that I learned through Gary Smalley's video series, "Keys To Loving Relationships." The material for this section comes from the session on "Using Emotional Word Pictures to Increase Intimacy and Understanding." Emotional word pictures are powerful in communicating our feelings including situa-tions that make us angry. As Gary states in his notes for the video series: "...using word pictures can help tap deeply into a person's emotions and see the greatest change." Word pictures are personalized stories that connect the other person with an event and lock this in his memory. With anger, emotional word pictures can help the other person feel our pain from what they did to us.

In the Bible, Nathan used a word picture with David to explain David's sin in 1 Samuel 12:1-10: "...*There were two men in a certain town, one rich and the other poor. The rich man had a very large number of sheep and cattle, but the poor man had nothing except one little ewe lamb he had bought. He raised it, and it grew up with him and his children. It shared his food, drank from his cup and even slept in his arms. It was like a daughter to him. Now a traveler came to the rich man, but the rich man refrained from taking one of his own sheep or cattle to prepare a meal for the traveler who had come to him. Instead, he took the little ewe lamb that belonged to the poor man and prepared it for the one who had come to him.' David burned with anger against the man and said to Nathan, 'As surely as the Lord lives, the man who did this deserves to die! Then Nathan said to David 'You are the man!'"* A story about a lamb would surely evoke an emotional response from David who had been a shepherd for many years. We see how God even uses word pictures effectively. Word pictures are developed from knowing the other person's interests and using an example to communicate our hurt feelings.

Topics to use for word pictures are:

1. The various components of nature—like water, animals, weather, etc.

2. Create stories that get the other's attention—create your own story.

3. Use common objects that are used all the time—like coffee pot, toys, cars etc.

4. Shared experiences with family members or friends.

Any one of the above can be used effectively to create a personal word picture. What makes it emotional is that the other person will immediately connect with the story told and its purpose. They will be able to "feel" your hurt from what they did and remember it. Because of this connection there is greater likelihood that they will not repeat the offense.

Gary lists the steps necessary to take to make an emotional word picture successful:

1. Define your purpose—with anger, it would be to help the other person understand the pain you have felt from their actions or their negative anger.

2. Understand the other person's interests—think of the other person's interests as the basis for your word picture.

3. Create the word picture from one of the four above concepts—use the other person's interests to select the best example.

4. Practice your word picture with a friend—this will create greater confidence when you use it.

5. Select a good time with few distractions—be patient and don't rush your presentation.

6. Need to be persistent in presenting the picture—avoid overusing word pictures with someone.

In angry situations, word pictures can be a very effective tool to help stop actions of someone else that has hurt us. Because they leave a lasting reminder in the person's mind about that particular incident, this creates a greater opportunity for more peaceful relations. Gary indicated that he taught this to all his family who use word pictures on him.

In summary, we have listed a number of important concepts that should be used in connection with RAA. These tools are so important that they can make the difference between success and failure. They represent the experiences I have gleaned from my classes at Teen Challenge and other authors on anger. I suggest that you try using them.

Summary:

Matthew: 18:15-17 process of dealing with anger between Christians.

Dealing with reversal
Using time outs to change the emotional situation
Avoiding angry people
Avoiding smiling when in an angry situation
Talking out our anger with a friend
Being aware of the distance factor with people
Creating emotional word pictures

Discussion Questions

1. Have you ever used Matt 18:15-17 in an angry situation? If so, what were the results? After reading this, would you use it?

2. What is a time out? Would you ever have a need to use it?

3. What is reversal? Have your ever encountered reversal in your angry situations?

4. Do you have angry friends? Has this affected your anger?

5. Have you ever talked out your anger with a friend? What were the results? Would you do it again?

6. What is the distance factor? Were you aware of it before reading this?

7. What is an emotional word picture?

Chapter 6
Conflict: A Path to Greater Intimacy

Conflict is defined as: "as a clash, competition, or mutual interference of opposing forces of ideas or interests." In our context, as expressed in various books on anger, conflict is an intense interaction between two or more people, where some form of anger is being expressed. Carolyn Schrock-Shenk and Lawrence Ressler in their book, *Making Peace with Conflict,* describe conflict as follows: "Ironically, conflict is an opportunity to know. Without conflict we tend to keep to ourselves carefully hidden from God and from others." Thus conflict, if handled positively, leads to deeper understanding of others. Additionally, conflict can open us up to new thoughts, which leads to emotional and mental growth.

Usually, one person starts the conflict by expressing anger, which often results in the other person responding in the same way. Accordingly, we see that conflict is composed of two or more people or groups opposing each other with some form of anger. Some people mistakenly interchange anger and conflict without distinguishing between them. Anger is not conflict when it is expressed against oneself, an object or not expressed by the person (stored anger). Also, anger expressed becomes a conflict only when the receiving person or group opposes them. If the receiving person(s) elects not to oppose them, then there is no conflict. In reality, most people will oppose an angry person in some angry way. This opposition will take one of two forms. It will either be positive conflict where positive anger is expressed and resolution is possibly reached, or negative conflict where negative anger is expressed and there is no resolution.

Usually, when we hear or see that a conflict is about to arise, many of us want to run from it, either emotionally or physically. In fact, just the thought of conflict can set one's stomach churning because we know that probably hostile anger (negative conflict) will be expressed. Usually loud voices and strong emotions are part of the conflict process. Anxiety is present because neither side knows how the conflict will turn out. We fear that relationships will be broken and bitterness (long-term anger) will be the conclusion. It has been said that conflict will end with either a "bitter or better" result for the relationship. Consequently, it seems to us like a big gamble to go into a conflict at all because the outcome many times is negative.

Therefore, fear often takes over and controls our actions and words in such circumstances. The usual ways to deal with conflict are negative as follows:

1. Flight from the conflict. We try to avoid the conflict by retreating into ourselves by denying our feelings to keep peace. This burying of our anger and emotions, however, will only last temporarily (as stated in Chapter Two on negative anger). It will come out inevitably, either in passive-aggressive ways, or it will become explosive anger.

2. Aggressive conflict. We attack using loud voices and strong words (even swear words) hoping to overpower our opponent. We want to win the conflict on our terms, allowing us to feel that we are in control. This action, we think, will make us feel better but in the end it never does. If there is a winner, then there is obviously a loser who can leave with revenge in his heart.

3. Combination of styles one and two, whereby one person attacks verbally and the other, to keep peace in the relationship, acquiesces to the attacker.

4. Distancing. Both parties, fearing aggressive anger, may resort to hostile silence as a way of expressing their discontent.

All four negative options usually result in a buildup of anger (bitterness) and a desire for even greater revenge. The cycle will not be broken until someone seeks help from God or a mature Christian, or changes to a positive conflict approach.

> Ed was an easygoing guy who lived with a volatile wife, Ruth. She had experienced a difficult childhood with abuse and pain, which she brought into the marriage. Her volatile anger took the forms of shouting and putdown words to Ed. She would use these methods to control the situation. Ed, to "make peace," would let her have her way. He feared such angry conflict and wanted it settled as quickly as possible. As a result of his fear, he would give into almost all her demands. He thought that his yielding would appease her and make her happy with him but just the opposite occurred. She continued with her angry outbursts. In reality, she lost respect for him. Ed's lack of forthrightness only made him feel worse about himself and lowered his self-esteem. Why couldn't he stand up to her? Not until she filed for divorce did he begin to realize that his inaction, like Hamlet, had led to a death. In this case, the death of a marriage.
>
> What Ed lacked was the courage and wisdom to break from his old unworkable pattern of behavior with conflict. Later, after several discussions with him, he realized his mistake. He changed his anger expression from stuffing anger to RAA.

This true story reflects opposite ends of the conflict cycle. At one end, Ruth expressed only her needs with no desire to relate while Ed tried to keep peace by suppressing his needs for the sake of the relationship. Such an imbalance is all too common in our relationships and only perpetuates a negative cycle of conflict. We need to strive to balance our needs and the importance of the relationship. When both of these needs achieve at least some satisfaction we will have more peace in our relationships.

In Job 3:25 we read: *"What I feared has come upon me; what I dreaded has happened to me."* Just like Job, we let fear control our actions and we become immobilized to the trials and challenges of life. We lack the knowledge of how to go through the conflict in a positive way to make things better. Our past experiences, learned either at home or in the world, has usually shown us only the negative results of conflict. Consequently, we mistakenly develop a "fight or flight" attitude. These opposite approaches lack the balance of respectful assertiveness and empathy needed to positively resolve conflict.

When we are in a conflict situation, we need to find ways that show respect toward each other. These respectful actions will create the opportunity to establish mutual dialogue, which Christ wants for all of us. We need to involve Him in the process. We call this positive conflict and it will result in emotional growth for both parties. It is the best way to deal with our angry emotions, which we know are inevitable in any relationship.

> Henry and Tyrone came into Teen Challenge separately from different cities. They were both in their twenties and seemed to be drawn together by their common interest in praying to God. Both of them would get up early to pray to God and read the Bible together. This bonding drew them close together so that they became close friends. One day Henry made a hostile remark about Tyrone's prayer, which Tyrone felt was a put down. Tyrone had been in my "Anger Reconciliation Class" and had learned how to use positive conflict. He started using the biblical principles that he had practiced in class to express his unhappiness to Henry about his remark. Henry's anger expression had been aggressive anger before he came into the TC program. Accordingly, it seemed a major conflict was about to erupt. Tyrone's approach

> defused that with his calm and caring way of explain-
> ing his anger. Henry, at first resisted apologizing. As
> the dialogue went on, he felt a Holy Spirit conviction,
> which caused him to want to apologize, which he did.

The causes of conflicts come from several sources:

Crisis situations. These may include those extremely stressful situations like: the death of a loved one, divorce, severe illness, severe emotional illness, jail for a family member, etc. Any of these circumstances
put great stress and potential conflict in any relationship. If there are
other underlying problems in the relationship, this additional stress
can easily cause conflict to flare up that can breakup the relationship
between participants.

> Jean was married to Phil, who was a drug addict. She
> had struggled for years with his addiction, but, being
> a Christian, she had stood by him. Phil came to Teen
> Challenge to get healed from his addiction. There, he
> made progress but during his stay his daughter, Sue,
> got very sick. Phil and Jean, along with everyone at
> Teen Challenge began praying for Sue. This action
> seemed to draw Phil and Jean closer together. How-
> ever, Sue's health faltered and she eventually died.
> The pain was devastating for both Phil and Jean.
> Finally, with the sting of the loss unhealed, Jean fell
> away and left the marriage. This action left Phil at a
> loss and he left Teen Challenge.

Selfish motives. Selfishness is defined as: "concern for ones' own wel-
fare or advantage at the expense of or disregard of others." This self-
centered approach in conflicts becomes apparent to the other person,
who resents it. In effect, we are disrespecting the other party, which
creates a conflict in itself. The Bible speaks strongly against selfishness

in Philippians 2:3: *"Do nothing out of selfish ambition or vain conceit, but in humility consider others better than yourselves."* Then again in James 3:16: *"For where you have envy and selfish ambition, there you find disorder and every evil practice."* These verses show that God's heart is for us to consider others' concerns and problems before our own. When we recognize others' concerns, we are able to connect with the other person and understanding is achieved. Even though we are born with the human condition of selfishness in our lives, God wants us to overcome this sin by thinking of others in our words and actions. Humility is the antidote for selfishness and is the quality God wants to see in us. Seeking humility enables us to develop ways to work together in unity.

> Edna felt strongly that her family, and even her extended family, should look only to her for advice. She told all the family members of her opinion. She felt an inner confidence that she had the experience and wisdom to meet their needs. However, when questioned by other members of the family, she got angry and defensive. This created resentment with some of the family, who didn't appreciate her selfishly controlling the situation. As a result, they resisted her counsel by not coming to see her. Selfishness excludes others while humbleness seeks others.

Attacks on our self esteem. When we are not given unconditional love while growing up, we tend to feel devalued as a person. In his book *Anger Trap* Dr. Les Carter clarifies this: ". . . that the message of unconditional love was not fully addressed, leaving a question mark in developing children's minds. Not knowing for certain if their worth was constant, these individuals learned to respond to conflict with an attitude of uncertainty." As a result, when their ideas are rejected, they tend to feel rejected as persons. This rejection leads to their getting angry with others when they don't agree with them or respect their opinions.

Sam grew up in a difficult home with an angry father who gave him no love and minimum attention. His father consistently put Sam down and degraded him during his growing up years. These actions left a lasting memory in Sam's mind. Later he married his wife, Sandy, who didn't understand his strong angry reactions when she challenged his opinion. This action would start a serious conflict between them. Sam's emotions would erupt and try to take control of the situation. Sandy felt at such a loss as to how to deal with Sam's strong emotions that she thought she would have to leave him. After evaluating her marriage situation, she told him that she would stay for the sake of the children. Unfortunately, Sam never changed and Sandy and their children continued to suffer from his temper.

Differences in values and personalities can many times provoke conflict as we try to convince others of the "correctness" of our values. As these are closely held values, they are significant to us and we feel compelled to fight for them. For Christians, this includes believing and asserting our love for Jesus and His principles. This fact alone can and does divide families into believers and nonbelievers. Luke 12:51 (NIV) states: *"Do you think I come to bring peace on earth? No, I tell you, but division. From now on there will be five in one family divided against each other, three against two and two against three."* In these verses Jesus tells us how families will have conflicts because of Him. Additionally, conflicts can occur over other controversial issues such as: abortion, political parties, homosexuality, swearing, smoking, etc. Our personality differences are often the sources of attraction as couples, but later they lead to irritation and conflict.

Generational anger. This negative anger that is expressed by one generation modeling it to the subsequent generation. Even though the pain caused by this anger is hated by the children, this daily teaching of negative aggressive anger is internalized. Later, if not corrected by God's intervention or therapy, the grown up children instinctively repeat the same deadly aggressive anger with the same painful conflict resulting. This same process continues from generation to generation until someone realizes the negative results and wants to change their anger expression.

> Larry came from a family where his father used explosive anger regularly on him and his other siblings. His father had been the victim of his own father's explosive anger and putdowns. Continuing this generational anger, his father was forever exploding in anger, creating conflict over some threat or frustration in his life. It seemed as if there was no peace in the family. Larry was intimidated by his father's seemingly uncontrolled shouting and even hitting. He wanted to get away as soon he became old enough to leave the house for college. There, to his surprise, he found that he had developed the same anger as his father, which caused him to erupt in the same destructive ways. His new-found aggressive anger seemed natural to him, making him the third generation to express anger in the same way. Later, he married and had a son to whom he continued to express the same destructive anger pattern with the resulting conflict in the family. This painful cycle of passing on generational anger can negatively affect literally hundreds of people.

We have seen the various causes of conflict, some of which may be your triggers. Maybe you have felt the pain of negative conflict and want to change. Just as we choose our anger expression, we also have a choice of our type of conflict—either positive or negative. The equation for negative conflict is:

Threat → anxiety → negative conflict → inflict pain on others → receive pain back; left alone; loss of relationships

If I choose positive conflict, I will probably have a far better chance of a positive resolution; however, that result is not guaranteed. The principles for positive conflict are similar to positive anger. They are as follows:

Bring God into the situation. This principle is critical since God does not create conflicts, but seeks to resolve them. Satan is the one that provokes conflicts because he wants dissension, which creates negative anger. We have several examples of God's people involved in conflict in the Bible: Paul and Barnabas over taking Mark on an evangelistic trip (Acts 15:37-39) and Aaron and Miriam questioning Moses leadership because of Moses' Ethiopian wife (Numbers 12:1-9). Accordingly, seeking God's answer in prayer over a conflict is vitally important as we submit to Him for help. He will send the Holy Spirit to work in both participants for mutual resolution. In reviewing the conflicts from the Bible, we see how God was able to use them for good. Mark later joined Paul and they did great ministry together. God condemned Aaron and Miriam for questioning the leadership of Moses and gave Miriam leprosy for seven days. Additionally, God told them both that Moses was His chosen leader. These actions confirmed that Moses was the rightful leader of the Israelites.

Respect. This means a high regard for someone and is reflected in our words and how we deliver them. This principle is most important to remember because, by our showing respect, the other person knows we care for him. Even in the heat of conflict, over time, the other person will soon grasp the esteem they are being shown and will respond more respectfully themselves. They are expecting disrespect back since that is what they are probably accustomed to receiving. Showing respect to the person, however, will open the door to real dialogue and mutual understanding. Our being respectful does not require agreement with someone else's point of view, but it does value their freedom to have a different point of view.

Seeking to listen. It is critical to listen to the other person because, in most cases, we only know our side of the story. Therefore if we act only on half of the story we probably are not dealing with the whole truth. Many times in a conflict, people talk over each other and never truly listen to what is said. They just want to vent their emotions and win the argument. In other words, they don't want really want to hear the other person's opinion as it might mean that they are wrong. However, by listening to what is said, we not only show respect, but the other person may realize this and start to listen to us. In order to achieve true understanding, we need to listen carefully to each other.

As we discussed on Chapter Three, the use of "reflective listening" emphasizes our desire to hear what is said (see p.52 for reflective listening definition). Again our listening does not guarantee that the other person will want to, or be able to listen to us.

Patience. Having patience with someone in a conflict is particularly important when that person is disrespectful and not listening. Lack of patience is typical of negative conflict, where the person is trying to force a conclusion of their ideas on the other person. This concept is discussed in the book, *The Anger Trap*, by Dr. Les Carter: "When conflict and aggravation arise, anger is expressed because of a desire for closure. The anger-producing circumstances represent an unwanted intrusion and the anger person immediately wishes to put an end to the disruption." This desire for conclusion on our terms only leads to resentment and no conclusion. As a result, there is a great need for patience and time to negotiate a mutually agreed upon solution. Our goal is to practice positive conflict and thereby reach mutual understanding. In Chapter One, we discussed how anger arises out of a threat or frustration. This action oftentimes produces hurt, which is expressed in the emotions of anger in conflict. We need to deal with these feelings by discussing them and empathizing with them, which creates connectedness. Connectedness with the person will develop as the person realizes we care not only for their ideas but their feelings as well. As we have discussed before in Chapters Three and Four, feelings are the pathway to beliefs. These feelings, however, may represent a true or false situation. We need, with Christ's help, to find and live in the truth, which brings freedom (like Jesus promised).

Create an atmosphere of security. Security is defined as: "freedom from danger." Achieving a feeling of security is a basic need of all humans and is especially strong in women. Without safety for both of the participants in a conflict, then no positive resolution is possible. The participant(s) will not take the risk to resolve the conflict if this basic need is not perceived to be possible. As the authors for *Design for Wholeness* state: "Often it is only in the secure and safe environment of an intimate friendship, spiritual direction, counseling or therapy that people will feel free enough to explore the meaning of their anger." Creating that safe environment where the participants feel that they won't be hurt or attacked is challenging. We can help by using our Christian principles listed above in working through conflict.

Willingness to compromise. This involves a desire to change your thinking if you find that the truth is different than what you thought. We all are called to make adjustments in our lives based on changes that occur from aging, different friends, different environments, etc. If we are inflexible we will have a difficult time with these changes. Thus when conflict arises we can be flexible enough to listen to other points of view, which can help resolve conflicts. We must, however, never compromise on our Christian faith and biblical principles.

By putting the seven principles together, we have positive conflict. We need to realize that positive conflict will not resolve every conflict, as most cannot be resolved without both parties seeking resolution. This situation is particularly true when one party, because of their own fears, lacks the patience for discussing the situation, or is selfishly caring only about themselves. Consequently, our expectations for resolution of conflicts need to be tempered with this reality. Nevertheless, we need to pursue positive conflict because of its many positive results as follows:

Clarity of ideas between people. Sometimes when people, even Christians, have different ideas, it may take conflict to sort out the best option. I have found that this is true in the groups where I am a member, whether it be the Church Board, the Men's Ministry, or my family. There can be a productive struggle to find the godly idea. This conflict will take time and patience to work through successfully. The results, however, are very rewarding once the ideas are arrived at mutually. These shared ideas usually work out the best.

Clarity of goals between people. Goals can be different for all of us because they set the path for our future actions. Different goals can easily divide people and groups and are reflections of the differences in the participants. Thus conflict arises, which has the potential to divide the participants. With positive conflict, we have the ability to arrive at mutually developed goals. While this goal may not please everyone, all participants have a sense of ownership in the final goal. As a result, they will be more inclined to help achieve the goals.

Clarity of expectations. One of the biggest obstacles to mutual contentment in a relationship is different expectations between the participants. Every one of us comes into a relationship with some similar and different expectations. Many times these expectations are our own selfish desires, which can easily lead to conflict because they are not shared expectations. Unless these differences are discussed before the marriage, they can result in problems in the relationship. If these different expectations are resolved positively, there can be a new vitality in the relationship.

The book *The Five Love Languages* by Gary Chapman discusses the different ways in which we can show love to our mate. In effect, they are like five ways of showing and receiving love from our mates. All five options are good, but one is particularly more significant to our mate. We need to discuss all these options with our spouses. Once we know our mate's love language (expectation of love), we can communicate to our mate their particular love language resulting in them feeling loved. Many times, couples don't know their partner's love language, which results in one party not feeling truly loved. Then conflict can arise.

> My wife originally thought that my love language was the various pies she made for me (the gift of service). She makes very good pies, but that was not my favorite love language. For years, she felt content to bake the pies for me, thinking that she was meeting my deepest need. However, after we both read, *The Five Love Languages,* and we discussed our own love language, she discovered that my favorite love language was "touch." Touch ranges from physical touching all the way to sex. Thereafter, she has definitely tried to meet my love language in that area. Her love language, I found out, was "spending time with me" which I try to meet. This mutual effort has made our relationship closer and deeper.

Most positive change does not happen without some conflict. Change in general is hard for most people and doesn't happen without being motivated. Conflict can provide that motivation since it brings out our strong feelings. By working through those feelings in a positive way, we can see that change in our lives is not only necessary, but positive. Conflict helps break through our basic inertia where we are comfortable with our present position. It allows us to see other sides and options. God wants us to change to be more Christ-like so He allows us go through trials and conflicts for a positive reason.

Creates greater intimacy with others. Going through a conflict with a person(s) in a positive way can develop a deeper relationship with that person. If I am holding back my anger due to fear of expressing it, I am also holding back expressing my full range of other emotions: real love, sadness, joy, happiness, etc. Consequently, if I allow my fears of expressing anger to hold me back from conflict, I am limiting my relationships to a superficial level. Andrew Lestor in *Coping with Your Anger* points this out: "You know that a relationship between two normal people, such as marriage partners or parents and children, is bound to spark some conflict. It is clear that when anger is dealt with openly and straightforwardly, it promotes (and even creates) intimacy." In the book, *Brothers!*, Geoff Gorsuch discusses in detail a relational diamond. Most of the following material, however, comes from classes that Promise Keepers taught on this principle.

Stage I: Acquaintances. This is an initial stage of relationship where we are reaching out to accept another person. There is a sharing information stage where we get to know each other better. We seek to build trust, which requires confidentiality between the persons. As we make these steps, our communication advances from being guarded to being more relaxed. Conflict is purposely avoided by both parties, because they don't know how it will affect the relationship. Most relationships stay at this stage because of fear of conflict and/or commitment.

Stage II: Friends. In this stage, each party seeks to draw closer to the other by developing a deeper understanding of the other. This, in turn, leads to greater trust and mutual respect. As a result, dialogue now includes the sharing of deeply held feelings and opinions. There is a mutual desire to encourage each other. For Christians, other signs of reaching this level may be mutual prayer and Bible reading as a regular part of the meetings. Confessions of wrongs and failures are made by both parties. A connectedness develops so that they eat meals together regularly and want to be together. To achieve this stage, they must have successfully gone through at least one conflict together. As a result, they break through the barrier that prevents true intimacy—

expressing their anger. Holding back on the inevitable conflict will result in the relationship stagnating at the acquaintance level, possibly forever.

> Ernie had known Mark from church and needed some carpentry work done on his house. Because of their initial good relationship, Ernie arranged with Mark to have the work done in two weeks. After the two weeks was up, Mark had not come to the house. Ernie called Mark and when he couldn't get him, he left a message. A week later Ernie called again and couldn't get Mark so he left another message. Later, at church, he saw Mark and questioned him why he hadn't called back. Mark explained that he had been too busy. The discussion got more heated and ended up in a conflict. Later Mark came and did a great job. While on the job Ernie spoke with Mark and they worked out their differences. This positive resolution led them to a greater friendship that continues to this day.

Stage III: Brothers/Sisters. This is the covenant stage of relationship where each party can hold the other accountable. They learn to work closely together on various projects. They help each other using their different strengths. There is a special bonding that has taken place where they can even sense the feelings of the other person. This connectedness allows each to truly share their heart's joys, sorrows and problems. Each wants to help the other with their trials and challenges. They do many activities together including worshipping God. If conflict arises, it is settled easily because of their mutual past positive experience in resolving conflict.

We can now see that getting through conflict positively is a critical step in the path of deepening a relationship. Handling conflict positively makes our relationships grow, which is why I entitled this chapter: "Conflict—A Path to Greater Intimacy."

I had a friendship for about four years with Abner where we would see each other on an occasional basis. We seemed to have developed an easy relationship that almost seemed like friends, but we had never gone through conflict together. Then one day Abner got angry at me for not supporting him at a particular time. His anger poured forth as he expressed his hurt at my lack of support. I realized that he was right and I admitted it and asked for his forgiveness. After a moment, he forgave me. I told him that I would support him in the future and that this was a mistake I wouldn't repeat. Thereafter, he had my support and, over time, he realized it. Our relationship grew much deeper and we support each other now all the time. Our relationship has grown from friends to brothers.

On the other hand, I have also seen the opposite where mishandling a conflict, using negative anger, can break a relationship.

My mother, Alex, got into a conflict with her sister, Chickie, after the death of their aunt. The aunt left all her possessions, not much at the time, to Chickie, with whom she had stayed for the last years of her life. This action incensed Alex, who had cared for the aunt previously for 10 years. Alex felt the aunt's love had been transferred to Chickie. Alex, using negative anger, accused Chickie of pressuring the aunt into changing her will. After the conflict, Alex and Chickie never spoke again and this relational rupture was transferred to us children for years. For example, our usually large family gatherings changed to exclude Chickie's family. The consequences from this painful conflict resulted in the family's breakup and I never again saw my aunt and her daughter.

We have reviewed the many benefits that positive conflict can have for us. Based on this, let us start using these principles for positive conflict all the time. The equation for positive conflict is:

Threat → anxiety → positive conflict → positive resolution → greater intimacy & positive change; clarity of goals, expectations & ideas

The following chart* from the book, *Making Peace with Conflict,* compares positive and negative conflict. I believe it demonstrates why positive conflict is so important for us to use.

Positive Conflict Traits	Negative Conflict Traits
1. People adjust, change, compromise.	1. People are rigid, inflexible, inconsistent.
2. People interact with an intent to learn.	2. People interact with intent to protect self and hurt the other person.
3. People do not stay stuck in a conflict.	3. People become stuck in their position.
4. Increased self-esteem in the participants.	4. Increased fear, anger and insecurity.
5. Increased motivation for positive connection with others.	5. "Fight pattern" (desire to destroy the other's arguments or the person) or "flight pattern" (avoidance and resentment).
6. Has mainly a relationship focus.	6. Seeks mainly own self interest (own needs).
7. Presence of empathy.	7. Use demeaning verbal and non-verbal communication.
8. Cooperative, consider all people equal.	8. Competitive and destructive, marked by domination and subordination patterns.

*Chart adapted from Making Peace With Conflict, *edited by Carolyn Schrock-Shenk and Lawrence Ressler. Copyright 1999 by Herald Press, Scottdale, PA 15683.*

This comparison demonstrates the importance of the relational component of positive conflict vs. the importance of my need(s) dominating under negative conflict. Healthy conflict involves compromise. As Gary Oliver and Carrie Oliver state in the book *Mad About Us:* "In the context of conflict, compromise means bargaining some personal needs for some relational needs."

Even when we try to resolve the issue but the other person in the conflict still seems bent on his or her own selfish ways, don't give up. God can turn the conflict around. We need to be aware, however, of the barriers to resolving conflict. Some of them, you'll see, are similar to the problems with using RAA. These barriers are as follows:

Pride is an excessively high opinion of oneself. It is also one of the greatest sins and leads to destruction (Proverbs 16:18). Unfortunately, a prideful person creates a significant problem in negotiating a mutual agreement because they think that their ideas should determine the solution. Thus, there is usually limited dialogue with no desire to listen to the other person.

Suggested strategy: If the other person is a believer, ask to pray together for God to find a solution. Try to point out what Christ would think of the person's pride. Suggest that both of you practice humbleness and self-control. With an unbeliever, pray individually for God's help, then seek what small opportunities you can find in the discussion that will overcome the other's resistance.

Problems with communicating. If someone cannot communicate their thoughts and feelings, this can severely inhibit dialogue in a conflict. In fact, this can often create frustration in both parties leading to greater conflict. As a result, mutual understanding is difficult to obtain.

Suggested strategy: great patience is required to go slowly with the person using reflective listening. With their permission, you may be able to help them complete their ideas. One needs to be cautious about this, as you can make them feel devalued. Encourage any positive steps the person takes in communicating feelings and ideas. I have found this technique to work.

Selfishness seeking control. Such actions to dominate the conflict by the offender can become distracting and anger producing to the offended party. Consequently, the offended party sees the disrespect and oftentimes loses his/her desire to resolve the conflict. The source of such power-seeking tactics is frequently an inferiority feeling in the selfish person.

Suggested strategy: Pray and ask God to take control. Suggest that both of you have time to speak in an uninterrupted fashion. Emphasize that desire to negotiate a mutually agreeable solution for both parties and thereby show the opposite of selfishness.

Emotions out of control. These expressions prevent the person from listening and understanding you. Such actions get frustrating because the conversation becomes one-sided as the person is primarily concerned about venting their feelings.

Suggested strategy: Use the "time out" principle discussed in Chapter Five, which can be very effective. With groups in conflict, this tactic will be harder to implement, but possible if Christians are involved.

Unwillingness to, or fear of, change reflects an inner insecurity about the person over the uncertainty that change brings. Usually this anxiety is developed in childhood over painful changes that have occurred in that person's life. That fear of change is carried into adulthood with consequences to everyone around that person.

Suggested strategy: Implement the negotiated change in smaller pieces so that the adjustment is smaller. Use a great deal of encouragement with the person about any change they make. This strategy, I have found, will make changes easier.

We have seen that these five barriers can be overcome with God's help and patience in each case. It is important to realize that all the barriers represent some internal fear that is probably a lie that needs exposure to the truth. Once exposed over time, that barrier will diminish.

We have seen how conflicts, which are a part of everyday life, need to be handled in a positive way, or a gradual eroding of the relationships can occur. On the other hand, using positive conflict we can greatly enhance our relationships. We need to remember that avoiding conflict can be the worst tactic we can take, as the conflict will then be resolved by outside forces not under our control. As a result, the final solution of such inaction is usually painful to all parties.

So let us commit to using positive conflict principles in all our conflicts.

Summary:

Conflict is the clashing of two opposing forces where anger is expressed.

Causes of conflict: crisis situations, selfish motives, attacks on self esteem, differences on closely held values and generational anger.

Types of conflict: positive and negative.

Positive conflict principles are: Using God, respect, patience, listening, trying to understand the other's feelings.

Positive conflict results in clarity of ideas, goals and expectations, any positive change and greater intimacy.

Barriers to resolution: pride, problems with communication, selfishness seeking control, emotions out of control and unwillingness to, or fear of, change.

Discussion Questions

1. What is conflict? How do you feel about conflict after reading this chapter?

2. What are some of the causes of conflict? Can you relate to any of these?

3. What are some of the principles of positive conflict? Have you ever used any of them?

4. What are some of the positive results of positive conflict? Did these surprise you?

5. What are some of the barriers to resolution?

6. Will you now use positive conflict vs. negative conflict?

Chapter 7
Taking Responsibility for Our Anger

Anger, whether positive or negative, is perceived as an unpleasant emotion for most of us. It is not an emotion that we look forward to experiencing. Unfortunately, we will incur the feelings of anger many times in our lifetimes. As a result, we need to find the best way to express our anger constructively to make life better for ourselves and those around us. We have seen over the previous chapters how we have a choice between positive and negative anger. I realize that many readers may never have previously known about positive anger and positive conflict before reading this book. Hopefully, by now, that lack of knowledge about positive anger has been eliminated. As we have discussed in previous chapters, we do have a choice of which anger expression to use—positive or negative.

In making that choice, we need to take responsibility to make the best choice (positive anger) for us and for our friends and families. Responsibility is defined as: "moral, legal, or mental accountability." Therefore, we have a moral accountability for how we express our anger. By choosing positive anger, we will receive a greater chance of resolving it and, hopefully, we will achieve reconciliation with the other party in the process. On the other hand, by selecting negative anger we reap the consequences of our actions with the resulting pain to us, as well as to those around us.

The Bible gives us a biblical example of taking responsibility for anger. Abigail takes responsibility for her husband's (Nabal) insult to David. By taking this action, Abigail, saved her household from possible slaughter at David's hand and saved David from taking revenge. The story is in 1 Samuel 25:14-34: *"One of the servants told Nabal's wife Abigail: 'David sent messengers . . . to give our master greetings, but he hurled insults at them. Yet these men were good to us. They did not mistreat us . . . they were a wall around us all the time we were herding our sheep near them . . . see what you can do because disaster is hanging over our master and his whole household. David had just said: '. . . He has paid back evil for good . . . . When Abigail saw David, she quickly got off her donkey and bowed down before David with her face to the ground. She fell at his feet and said: 'My lord, let not the blame be on me alone . . . Now since the Lord as kept you, my master from bloodshed and from avenging yourself with your own hands, . . . And let this gift, which your servant has brought to my master, be given to the men who follow you. Please forgive your servant's offense, . . . David said to Abigail, '. . . May you be blessed for your good judgment and for keeping me from bloodshed this day and from avenging myself with my own hands.'"* Like Abigail, we have the responsibility to stop the consequences of negative anger. We too can learn from Abigail that sincere humbleness can significantly help to resolve anger.

Some of the characteristics of responsibility for our anger choice are:

Courage to try positive anger. Courage is defined as: "mental or moral strength enabling one to venture, persevere, and withstand danger, fear or difficulty firmly and resolutely." When we act with courage, there is no retreating from our belief in positive anger. We are asked by God to stand resolutely for our strongly held beliefs, particularly our Christian convictions. Our society today needs more courage from its Christian members. Our children need to see the example of their parents standing firm for what is right and true.

Ed Cole, in *Maximized Manhood,* writes of the need for men to act courageously: "Courage is the virtue, quality, or attribute of life that enables a man to face disapproval, persecution, fear, failure, and even death with a real manliness." Both men and women will need to exercise courage to use positive anger and overcome the pressures to stay with negative anger.

Do you have the courage to use RAA as your anger expression

even if it seems hard? God will hear us when we sincerely seek Him in our time of anger. He is there to exhort us to have courage to change our old sinful anger into a godly anger (positive anger) that will yield the fruit of righteousness. In the Bible, there are several times that God exhorted various leaders to have courage: Moses (Deuteronomy 31:6), Joshua (Joshua 1:6 and 10:25), Hezekiah (2 Chronicles 9:11), Esther (Esther 8:1-3), Peter (Matthew 14:27) and Paul (Acts 23:11). In each case, God helped each leader to overcome great difficulty. In fact, every great leader must have a large measure of courage to succeed. If God can give these leaders courage, He will do the same for us if we let Him. When God is with us He gives us His power to overcome, His presence to sustain us during the trial and His promises to succeed. In the book *Design for Wellness* the importance of courage is presented: "When a person is courageous and deals with anger it can be a source of life." Consequently, we need, for our own emotional and physical health, to be courageous in trying to use positive anger expressions, especially RAA.

> Doug faced a difficult situation, as his wife suddenly wanted a divorce. He urgently needed to have some time off from his job to deal with this situation. His boss, whom he had known for over seven years as a good friend, was giving Doug a difficult time by not responding to his telephone calls. This seeming rejection left Doug at a loss to understand why this was happening, given their long-term relationship. Doug's anger was boiling when we talked about it. I encouraged him (gave him courage) to utilize the principles of RAA, one of which is patience. His main anger expression was stuffing his anger so he was not skilled and did not have experience with confrontation.
>
> Nevertheless, he called his boss again and was able to get an appointment with him. Then he told me how he was fearful of meeting his boss and didn't want to go. We prayed again to God and Doug

received new courage to face his boss. With his new-found courage, Doug asserted not only his need but also his hurt at how the boss had avoided him. His boss apologized and gave him the days he needed. Doug was so happy with the results that he has continued to use RAA in angry situations. Additionally, his faith in God has also grown stronger.

Convicted to use positive anger. Conviction is defined as: "the act of convincing a person of error or of compelling the admission of a truth." When I get convicted by my negative anger expression, the Holy Spirit causes me to seek repentance and God's forgiveness for my action. This action has caused me to make changes in my anger expression. Being convicted brings us from being outside God's will with our negative anger back into God's will with positive anger. Consequently, when we make a mistake with our anger expression with someone, we need to confess that to the person and to God. He will send His Holy Spirit with healing for us.

> Many years ago when I was living in New York City, I used hostile anger with my sister in a telephone conversation. I blamed her for doing something that I thought she did wrong. (I don't remember the exact details after 46 years). My demands were unreasonable and my words were hurtful. I know that I caused her to start crying. As soon as we finished talking, I felt such a heavy conviction in my heart. I cried out, "Dear God please forgive me for I have sinned." Later I apologized to her and I have treated her with respect in our consequent interactions so our relationship was restored.

God's corrective influence, the Holy Spirit, helps us change our ungodly anger and provide healing resolution. As a result of His involvement in my particular situation, I found peace in my heart. This result compares to negative anger where conviction becomes self-guilt leading to depression.

Commitment to use only positive anger expression. Commitment is defined as: "the act of committing to the charge, keeping, or trust." We see that commitment means we put all our trust in using positive anger and give up any trust we had in negative anger. In effect, I am entrusting any of my anger expressions to God's direction. This action is a moral choice on my part to be bound to use positive anger, especially RAA, when expressing anger. In I Samuel 7:3 (NIV), Samuel describes commitment: *"And Samuel said to the whole house of Israel, 'If you are returning to the Lord with all your hearts, then rid yourselves of the foreign gods and the Ashtoreths and commit yourselves to the Lord and serve him only . . .'"* Here Samuel is talking about a spiritual commitment, but the same concept applies to our commitment to use only positive anger expression.

Any long-lasting commitment is grounded in keeping our strong beliefs. These enabled the early Christians and those persecuted today to withstand torture and even death. 1 Peter 4:19 (NIV) states: *"So then, those who suffer according to God's will should commit themselves to their faithful Creator and do good."* Thus, while we may be doing right by choosing positive anger, the other person may still choose to inflict pain on us with negative anger. The point of the verse is to keep using positive anger and He will support us through the suffering. In the end, God will use the suffering to help us to stay humble and He will prevent us from adopting the lie that negative anger will work better than positive anger. We also know that continuing to express positive anger will create a climate for reconciliation, even if it takes time.

A suggested prayer might be: *Dear God, I am pledged to use positive anger expression all the time regardless of the immediate cost. I trust you, Jesus, to restore broken relationships in your time.*

Kenny was a bright 17-year-old student at Teen Challenge. He came from a family that did not enforce boundaries on Kenny as he grew up. As a result, Kenny got into drugs at 13 and progressed to more dangerous drugs as he aged. This brought him to Teen Challenge and to my class. There he saw RAA practiced but he was unruly and didn't want to learn it. This bad attitude got him into trouble as he would not respect authority. After being disciplined several times, the staff got fed up and sent him for a week to the Syracuse Rescue Mission.

There he saw the hard side of life and started really reading his Bible. At the Rescue Mission, I talked with him when he attended my Bible study and I found he had developed a new commitment to change his life. He came back to Teen Challenge a new man resolved to submit to the rules and authorities. This changed attitude was reflected in my "Anger Reconciliation" Class where he demonstrated his new commitment by learning and using RAA very well. Kenny graduated and has gone on to lead a Christian life.

Determination to choose positive anger. The definition of determination that is appropriate for this section is: "the act of deciding definitely and firmly esp. a course of action." When we decide firmly on our anger expression, we have a sense of purpose behind our action—to find a way to get better results from our angry situations. In effect, we will not be swayed from this purpose by our emotions, past family history of negative anger, or other people's negative anger to us.

In Luke 9:51 (NIV), we see Jesus' determination: *"As the time approached for him to be taken up to heaven, Jesus resolutely set out for Jerusalem."* We see Jesus determined to get to his destination to accomplish his reason for coming to earth. We need the same dedication with commitment to use positive anger expression. God is calling us to avoid negative anger and use positive anger. Once other people real-

ize our resolution to use only positive anger, they too will feel pressure
to change their negative anger expression.

> Terry was a 32-year-old father who got into drugs
> while on the job. He was from Long Island where he
> had tried to go through the Teen Challenge pro-
> gram, but was unsuccessful because he was so close
> to his old neighborhood. To get away from the old
> influences, he was sent to Syracuse. Terry was bright
> and articulate in expressing himself. When he first
> came into my class, he expressed skepticism of the
> usefulness of RAA for him. Nevertheless, he learned
> it well and practiced it several times successfully in
> my class. His verbal ability helped him to state the
> necessary principles very well. Still, despite his profi-
> ciency at practicing RAA, Terry continued to doubt
> its usefulness for his life.
>
> Terry graduated and went on to the second
> phase of the program where he was with 250 other
> men versus only 15 in Syracuse. He wrote the follow-
> ing to Syracuse Teen Challenge after two months
> there: "Jim Offutt's class has, believe it or not, come
> in handy—I never thought it would. There is a
> whole lot of need for RAA when you live with 250
> guys! And yes, you have to exercise self-control. RAA
> is being put to the test and prevailing thank God!"
> Therefore, Terry's determination to use RAA, despite
> his own questions, has proved to be valuable—both
> to him and others.

EMOTIONAL SATISFACTION

When positive steps are used in a conflict and resolution is found for
both parties it is not unusual to feel an emotional high from the expe-

rience. This is especially true when there has been fear of confronting the person with whom we have had conflict. In reality, when we allow fear to control our lives and actions, we place ourselves in a dependent role. Our self-esteem becomes fragile and we feel weak when conflict arises. Since conflict is inevitable, instead of facing it, we avoid it. This pattern results in our denying our own deep needs to "keep the peace at any cost." Unfortunately, many times, the price for denying these important needs may lead to self-destructive behaviors such as: heavy drinking, use of drugs, depression and even suicide. However, once we break through the controlling fear to achieve success using the positive conflict steps there is an emotional relief and joy. At that point, we will have found a new successful way to overcome our fear of conflict, which has paralyzed us for so long. We need to remember the success and continue to use the positive steps whenever conflict arises until it becomes natural for us.

> Eric, an 18-year-old New Yorker, came up to me after my class at Teen Challenge and told me that he didn't believe that positive anger could work for him in his conflicts with other students. He stated that his situations were different than the other students who had used it successfully. I could see that he lacked the confidence to use positive anger because he was afraid of failing if he tried it. Later, in a following class, he erupted with anger at another student because he had bottled it up inside. I asked him at the break to try practicing the steps of positive conflict with his antagonist in class. He reluctantly agreed. At the onset, when he started the process, he had a serious and unfriendly expression on his face. He continued, however, and though it was a little rough in places, he succeeded in resolving the problem with the other student. The class applauded his effort, which caused him to smile and say: "This really does

work!" It was obvious that he was greatly relieved and a big weight had been taken off his shoulders.

The above components of being responsible for our anger expression require us to explore and modify our own values. It is what we believe that will determine our actions when an angry situation arises. I felt it is important, therefore, to review the different results between positive and negative anger. I have repeated the chart from Chapter One, but I added to it to reflect other characteristics of taking responsibility for our anger:

Characteristics	Positive Anger	Negative Anger
1. Spiritual	God controlling: use biblical principles to resolve.	God is not used: depends on self or worldly ideas.
2. Respect	Care is shown others in voice, words, and actions.	Disrespect is prominent in speech and volume.
3. Listening	Tries hard to listen and to understand the other person.	Usually does not hear or want to hear the other person.
4. Control	Tries to let God control. Seeks best for both parties.	Seeks self-control for own purposes.
5. Attitude	Confidence in words and actions.	Fear of others and what to do.
6. Feelings and experiences	Evaluated based on God's principles.	Evaluated based on how feelings.
7. Goal	Seeks to resolve the issues to make the relationship better.	Seeks to win: doesn't care about the relationship

As we can see above, the results for positive anger expression are far better for us and others in every category. Now, it is our responsibility to analyze these results carefully, and choose which type of anger expression is best for us, our families and friends.

For this next section, I am indebted to Andrew Lestor and his book *Coping with Your Anger*. Taking responsibility involves several steps set forth below:

Being aware of our anger. This is the first necessary step to finding resolution for our anger. It requires us to become sensitive to our feelings, not only of anger, but all our feelings. If we don't or won't recognize and connect with our anger, we will never be able to be responsible for it. This recognition will probably require us to change old habits of reaction to threats or frustrations. Such awareness may not be easy as we get older because they have become familiar and comfortable to us. Consequently, they are not easily changed. Christians oftentimes adopt stuffing their anger because they mistakenly believe that that is the only responsible way to deal with their anger as a Christian. Anger is energy; physics tells us that it must be expressed (released) some time and in some way. Sometimes, the wrong expression occurs, not at the time or place of our choosing, but in a public setting, which can be very embarrassing—if not to the angry person, at least for those witnessing the event (i.e. a woman shouting at her toddler in the grocery store).

As someone who stuffed his anger, I found that I had to listen and learn from the obvious signs of anger in myself—like a churning stomach. Also, I needed to recognize these signs of anger in others listed below, so I could deal with them. Therefore, identifying the following signs of anger will help us become more aware of them:

Physical manifestations. Clenched fists, headaches, a tightening of the muscles in the neck and face, chest pains, stomach problems, gastrointestinal problems and sudden increases in heart and breathing rates can be indicators of anger. Each person has distinct physical signs that can reveal their anger. Some of these physical signs may have another source other than anger like sickness. Accordingly, if we look for signs when we know we are angry we can learn to recognize our physical precursors to anger in us. Likewise, we need to identify the physical signs of anger in others, especially those close to us.

When one of these signs arise, ask yourself: Do I feel angry? Or, are they angry?

Emotional manifestations. Disappointment, depression, frustration, sullen, very sensitive, withdrawn, moody and sarcastic comments. Disagreeable attitudes can also be clues that indicate possible anger. Although these feelings may sometimes not be triggered by anger, other times they are. As a result, when these feelings arise, we need be honest and search ourselves for possible anger.

There are also issues which incite anger in us and others such as: seeking control, undue dependencies on others or substances, pride and inferiority feelings. In effect, we may be in bondage to these issues until we can resolve them. Therefore, we do need to ask ourselves these questions: Are we angry about something? Can we identify the cause?

Behavioral manifestations. Excessive eating, television, exercise, reading, and laughter all indicate a certain anxiety, which we know is the precursor to anger. When we see ourselves doing any of these things, check into: Am I doing any of these things to excess because I'm angry?

> George, a 25-year-old new student at Syracuse Teen Challenge, was looking down while sitting in my "Anger Reconciliation Class." As I gradually focused in on him, I noticed he had a frown on his face. Later, I noticed he had crossed his legs and arms so that he looked all closed up. George made no attempt to participate in the class so I called on him with a question. He didn't want to respond so I told him that I wanted to see him at the break. After some prodding, he finally told me that he had been hurt by another student's continued hostile comments and that he

was just angry. We talked about carefronting the other student and how to use RAA. After class I prayed with him and explained how he could use RAA. Later he tried RAA and it seemed to work as the comments stopped from the other student.

We need to be alert when one or more of the above signs occur in us or others. The greater the frequency of these signs, the greater the probability of anger. When we conclude that there are signs of anger, we arrive at the next step.

Labeling our feelings. We need to take ownership of our angry feelings by labeling them. By identifying our feelings, we can't ignore them and thereby keep the event in our memory. We do this by expressing words like: "I feel frustrated . . . disappointed . . . hurt . . . threatened . . . or irritated." In *Coping with Your Anger* Andrew Lestor states this clearly: "To name something in yourself not only helps you to recognize its existence but forces you to claim it as your own. Naming your anger facilitates taking responsibility for it." Labeling these feelings helps us to avoid forgetting about the incident. It becomes fixed in our memory. This action is particularly necessary for people who stuff their anger. Once we have ownership of our angry feeling(s), then we can move on to the next step.

Praying and understanding our anger. This step is similar to one of the steps of RAA, where we seek God's understanding and direction in dealing with our anger. He helps us to center and control our reactions to angry events so that we respond with positive anger and avoid negative anger. Most people fail to get resolution because they respond out of their own emotions and/or their own understanding. We need to seek God's wisdom and thereby gain understanding as set forth in Proverbs 4:7: "*Wisdom is supreme; therefore get wisdom. Though it cost all you have, get understanding.*" Then we shall know what responsible action(s) to take with our anger. Andrew Lestor in *Coping with Your*

Anger points out that the power to our angry feelings is inside ourselves: "It is easy to blame other people, or groups, or events for our anger. However, this misses the real source, which is inside our own self." Often times the offending person has touched on the same feelings as our painful memory, which makes the pain stronger. Healing of this painful memory is the goal of Theophastic prayer.

Responding responsibly. If we have completed all the three preceding steps, then we are prepared to respond in a godly responsible way. We strongly recommend using the positive anger expressions as shown in the RAA method. Additionally, as we discussed in Chapter Three, there are critical parts to expressing our anger so as to create a climate for dialogue, mutual understanding and mutual resolution.

We see that these steps give us a plan to deal with our anger in a responsible mature way. You may want to start with a simple prayer: *Lord help me to try new steps in my life that will help me to be godly with expressing my anger.*

Even when we try these steps, there can be barriers inside ourselves that can hold us back from completing them. The obstacles that prevent us from being responsible for our anger include:

Making excuses. Excuse is defined as: "to try to remove blame from: seek indulgence for." Therefore, we see that people who use excuses for their anger are really actively avoiding any blame. The root of excuses can be pride or a fear of consequences. Using rationalizations to justify our anger is the opposite from taking responsibility for our anger expression. Using excuses is a childlike response, which avoids the challenges of adulthood. In Judges 6:14-16, the Lord tells Gideon: *"The Lord turned to him and said, 'Go in the strength you have and save Israel . . .' 'But Lord,' Gideon asked, 'how can I save Israel? My clan is the weakest in Manasseh, and I am the least in my family.' The Lord answered, 'I will be with you . . .'"* The Lord tells Gideon that his weaknesses are no excuse for how God can use him. Likewise, we have no excuse for not trusting God to help us when we use positive anger, RAA specifically.

Regrettably, it has become common place in our society for us to use excuses to condone our wrong actions. We try to prevent ourselves from facing difficult consequences in our lives—including facing our negative anger expression. Some of these excuses include: difficult family relationships, abuse, physical and emotional handicaps, poverty of love and material needs etc. While all of these may have left hurts and scars on us into adulthood, we have a choice of allowing those past hurts to control our future actions and anger expression. God can help us to use those scars for good. My own work in men's ministries, I believe, comes from my difficult relationship with my father, which caused me to want to help other men. Romans 8:28 exemplifies this concept: *"And we know that in all things God works for the good of those who love him, who have been called according to his purpose."*

Wanting revenge more than resolution. Our human reaction to being hurt causes us to want to strike back at the offender. That is revenge as we seek to get even for our hurt. Forgiveness is the last thing on our minds as that seems too good for the offender. God, however, in Romans 12:19 takes an opposite viewpoint: *"Do not take revenge, my friends, but leave room for God's wrath, for it is written: 'It is mine to avenge, I will repay, says the Lord.'"* God knows that seeking revenge instead of resolution will oftentimes lead us into bitterness as a result of holding our anger in for a long time. In effect, we allow Satan to use our unresolved anger to inflame our spirit with hate. When this happens, we become bitter in spirit, words and actions. God warns us against revenge in Hebrews 12:15: *"See to it that no one misses the grace of God and no bitter root grows up to cause trouble and defile many."* Therefore, bitterness is dangerous not only to us, but to others. It is Satan's way of spreading hate, whereas God wants us to work together for mutual resolution. In *The Anger Trap* Les Carter expresses the destructiveness of bitterness: "Usually the choice of bitterness allows them to feel temporarily powerful, but it also blinds them from seeing how their good qualities erode, and they eventually become a shell of their optimal selves."

Too comfortable to change. Human habits are commonplace with most of us, so changing our anger expression can be hard and uncomfortable to do. In *The Anger Workbook* Dr. Les Carter and Dr. Frank Minirith write: "We can go back to it again and again, not because we particularly like the anger, but because it is such a familiar part of our routine." This habit was learned in childhood and repeated countless times thereafter. Consequently, we continue to make the wrong choice with our anger even when we know better and the results are bad.

How do we overcome our subconscious urge to use negative anger?

Suggested Solutions: Bring these barriers to God in prayer and ask for Him to help break down these barrier(s) in you. By drawing close to Him and His word, we can gain the wisdom and strength necessary to correct these problems. Change will also require us to be determined to want to change these defensive ways. Showing respect in our interactions with others in conflict will help us to overcome fear and negative anger. Such an attitude of caring for the other person will help create a final resolution of the conflict.

Taking responsibility for our words and actions is a critical part of growing up and becoming mature spiritually and emotionally. Mature is defined in our case as: "having or expressing the mental and emotional qualities that are considered normal to an adult socially adjusted human being . . . fullness of growth." Accordingly, we need to fully develop our anger expression. An important part of achieving maturity is when we understand the difference between good and evil. Then, we know how to express our anger in a righteous way. Maturity is set forth in Hebrews 5:13-14 (NIV): *"Anyone who lives on milk, being still an infant, is not acquainted with the teaching about righteousness. But solid food is for the mature, which by constant use have trained themselves to distinguish good from evil."* Therefore, let us ask God to help us choose His anger expression for us.

We have previously discussed how negative anger is basically a childlike anger that we first use as babies. Growing up, we start to make our own decisions, which are often based on what we saw in our parents. Later, our choices become better as we learn from God and our experiences, but many times we stay with our same childhood negative anger. This strange dichotomy exists in many adults. Having read thus far, we know the full range of choices for our anger expression. Consequently, we now have the opportunity to make the mature choice for our anger expression. Taking responsibility also means accepting the consequences for our choice of anger expression, which is another aspect of maturity. Therefore, acknowledging our mistakes leads to emotional growth.

We too will make mistakes with our anger expression by using negative anger. The key is to confess our error to God and the person we offended so we do not repeat it.

> Thelma grew up in a normal middle class family. While young, she exhibited a strong hostile anger, which emerged only occasionally. Her parents were quiet people who, fearing her anger, would avoid her when she would go on one of her angry tirades. They did not try to set any boundaries on her anger so she felt free to express her hostile anger whenever she wanted. Once in school, she found she had to conform but occasionally her anger would boil over nonetheless. Thelma's anger kept her emotionally in a childlike state. The consequence of her hostility was that she had no real friends. People wanted to stay away from her because of her hostility. In effect, Thelma was in bondage to her emotions, which controlled both her words and actions.
>
> Later she met Walt, a quiet guy, who was attracted to the emotional fire in her personality. Walt held his anger in so that, in effect, they were a couple with anger opposites. As we know oftentimes opposites attract. However, this disparity in their anger created a situation where Thelma would get angry and get

her demands met while Walt, fearing hostile conflict, would give in. Thelma lived in constant depression and felt out of control with her emotions. Her children wanted to stay away from her because of her uncontrolled hostility.

This situation went on for years until Thelma decided that she wanted a divorce. Walt was both hurt and shocked by this event. Hadn't he given her everything she asked for? Why would she want a divorce? Walt struggled with the pain. With help from his friends and therapy, he began to express his anger to Thelma with more assertiveness and was less timid with conflict. This action improved his self-esteem and gave him the needed confidence to express his valid needs and values. Walt's attitude became more optimistic and his fears of Thelma's anger lessened. Meanwhile, Thelma continued in her hostile way and sunk into greater depression and even into drugs.

We see two different people, both with negative anger expressions. Once pressure is applied to them, one took responsibility for his anger and changed by using more positive anger, which yielded better results. The other person continued using negative anger despite worsening results and suffered greater pain, which hurt those closest to her.

Another consequence of our choice of anger expression is the modeling we show others—especially our children. Modeling in this case is defined as: "a person or thing regarded as worthy of imitation." We don't necessarily choose to be a model for our children but they are always studying us to learn what adults do. As a result, we, in effect, are always teaching them through our words and behavior. If these two give opposing messages, our behavior tells our children the real story. In effect, we become hypocrites to them whether we like it or not. Accordingly, when we model negative anger, but tell them not to do the same, children see through us and question which type of anger they should choose. Most likely, they will choose the same type of anger that we use. Thereby, children fail to learn about the empowerment of positive anger and its constructive results. In effect, the children will continue the generational curse of negative anger. Also we are modeling our anger expression to others around us who may look to us as role models. Often we fail to show others the redeeming power of confessing our mistakes and learning from them. Consequently, we need to take timeout to reflect on how we express our anger:

Is my anger expression what God has directed for me?

Do I find it successful in conflicts?

Should I take responsibility and change it?

Do I admit my mistakes and seek to change my behavior?

The answers to these questions will help us to make the right and best choice of our anger. Then we need to take corrective action with our expression of anger. We also need to understand that taking no action is also a decision as we let events make the decision for us. Taking no action is the weakest form of decision making and reflects a fear on our part in making difficult decisions and making the necessary corrections.

> My father grew up with a father who wouldn't face life with its demands. As a result, his father, my grandfather sought help from alcohol, which made him unemployable and unable to support his family. He expressed his anger explosively by breaking things and shouting uncontrollably. These actions forced my dad to leave his family at 10 years old and live with two maiden aunts. Later at school, he developed a stuttering problem because he was left-handed and his teachers forced him to write with his right hand. He didn't want to leave his mother who loved

him and he longed for her affection. The two aunts lived nearby so, fortunately, he was still able to see his mother frequently. However, my grandfather did not show any desire to relate to my dad. Consequently, he received no real male modeling in his life and lacked the confidence to relate with other men.

Despite all these problems, my dad took responsibility for his life and was able to graduate from the local college. He went on to MIT getting a BS and MS in Chemical Engineering. Later, he got married and was responsible as a provider for his family, unlike his father. Unfortunately, he did, however, carry a painful legacy from his father's aggressive anger. My dad never mastered his anger, although he got better as he aged. Despite his lack of positive modeling from his father, James did better in doing things with me, his only son. However, he did struggle to show affection to me.

When my son was born I really wanted to break that unhealthy pattern so I committed myself to relating to him and showing him affection from the time he was a baby. Also, I changed my anger expression to model RAA. I tell my son that he has the opportunity to improve the family model with his young family.

As a result, the family modeling has been turned from a "lemon into lemonade" because of taking responsibility for our lives, particularly with our anger. However, this progress can easily be lost by a descendent becoming irresponsible and starting a negative model using negative anger.

We all leave a legacy of how to handle anger to our children and grandchildren—whether we choose to do so or not. Think about your anger expression, is that what you want to pass on? If not, then now is the time to change!

Therefore, the importance of conveying a godly model to the next generation is critical to the establishing and/or continuing of a generational blessing of positive anger. Such a blessing is what God wants for us, our children and grandchildren. Likewise, we have the choice of passing along a generational curse of negative anger to future generations. Our anger expression is a part of the curse or blessing we pass on.

Do I want to pass on my curse of negative anger to future generations? Am I willing to break the curse of negative anger from previous generations? If so, Lord guide me to break that curse so that I can be a blessing by using positive anger in my relationships!

When I have tried my best using RAA but no change occurs: It can seem very frustrating when I have tried all the positive anger principles listed above yet no change occurs. In fact, things seem to get worse as the other person elects to stop interacting with us and retreats into hostile silence. This painful event happens in families all the time especially when our Christian values clash with worldly values. If all communication ceases, as what happened with my mother and her sister, our only real option is to give the other person up to the Lord and pray for them. The pain of such an event divides families and tests our true faith in God. Discussing this pain with God and/or a trusted Christian friend can reduce such pain. As we Christians know, God can take a long time to act and we know that the trials of life may bring back our wayward child or relative to us. Then we may be given God's opportunity to relate to them again. This is truly trust in God and His plans for us and the other party.

Taking responsibility for our anger expression is critical if we are to ever change from negative anger to positive anger. From the previous chapters, we have the information on positive anger we need to make a responsible choice. The question is: do we have enough desire to change our negative anger? If so, having the courage and determination are critical elements that we need to effect such a change. Making conscious attempts to change now begins with the steps of responsibility starting with being aware of our anger and then labeling it. By following these steps at our own pace, we can make progress with changing our anger expression. The principles in this chapter are sound and biblical so they will work over time. Consequently, while change can be difficult and frustrating, we need to have patience to see God work. We know this promise from God in Isaiah 55:11: *"so is my word that goes out from my mouth: It will not return to me empty, but will accomplish what I desire."* So we pray and trust in the Lord for change in our anger expression.

If you get frustrated with the slowness of change, ask yourself: Do I remember the pain and frustration from using negative anger?

Summary:

Responsibility is legal, moral, or mental accountability.

Characteristics of responsibility for our anger choice:
    Courage to try positive anger
    Convicted to use positive anger
    Commitment to use positive anger
    Determination to choose positive anger

Steps for taking responsibility for our anger:
    Being aware of our anger. The signs of anger are:
    Physical manifestations
    Emotional manifestations
    Behavioral manifestations
    Labeling our feelings
    Praying and understanding our anger

Maturity is attaining fullness of development.

Also understanding the difference between good and evil.

Modeling is a person or thing regarded as a worthy of imitation.

Start a generational blessing vs. a generational curse.

Discussion Questions

1. What does it mean to take responsibility for our choice of anger expression?

2. What is your choice of anger expression? Are you happy with it?

3. Define courage? Do you use courage in your daily life?

4. What is commitment? What is determination? Do you use these?

5. What are the steps of responsibility? Are you using any of them now?

6. What is understanding our anger about?

7. Describe the way I should respond in an angry situation? How do I actually respond?

8. What is maturity with my anger?

9. What does modeling my anger mean? What kind of model am I now?

10. What type of generational legacy am I passing on with my anger?

Epilogue

Anger occurs in everyone's life in one form or another. It has such a powerful effect on us that it can even become a bondage greater than drugs. Over my 15 years at Teen Challenge and in my own family, I have seen how negative anger can take control of a person's life with devastating results. Consequently, it is imperative that we learn to express anger in a constructive way. Otherwise, anger can literally destroy us and those around us. Accordingly, we need to be responsible by becoming aware of our anger, understanding it and articulating it in positive ways to others. Positive anger composed of: righteous anger, dropping anger (including forgiveness) and Respectful Assertive Anger (RAA) provide the constructive means to communicate our anger. A critical part of this process is that we come to God in prayer seeking His direction and calmness in expressing our anger. This is the way we break the potential bondage negative anger can have on us.

With violent anger on the rise in our families, communities and nation, we need to develop more dialogue on productive ways to deal with people's angry feelings. Teaching our youth about how to use positive anger in their lives is so important to all of us parents and grandparents. Learning and using RAA and forgiveness of anger comfortably in our lives can provide the necessary positive anger model that our youth need.

Lord, help us to persist in modeling positive anger to our spouses, children, friends and others even when others don't respond in a positive way with us! Give us the courage, commitment and determination to practice RAA and forgiveness with others, knowing that these biblical principles will prevail over the long-term. Help us to avoid the curse of negative anger but rather leave a blessed legacy of positive anger with future generations.

Notes

Chapter 1
Anger Is?

1. Andrew Lester, *Coping with Your Anger* (Westminster Press 1983) p. 92.
2. Ibid. p. 95
3. Loughlan Sofield. Juliane Carrel, Hammett Rosine, *Design for Wellness* (Notre Dame, Indiana: Ave Press 1990) p.27
4. Dr. Les Carter and Dr. Frank Minirith, *The Anger Workbook* (Nashville, Tennessee: Thomas Nelson, Inc. 1993) p. 17.
5. Ibid. p.14.
6. *Life Application Bible*-NIV Note for Ephesians 4:31, p. 2537
7. Ibid. Ephesians 4:26-27 p. 2537

Chapter 2
Negative Expressions of Anger: A Path to Pain

1. Dr. Les Carter, *The Anger Workbook* p.27.
2. Lestor, *Coping* p.52.
3. Ibid. p. 64.
4. Dr. Les Carter, *The Anger Trap* (Market Street, San Francisco, California, Jossey-Bass 2003) p. 26.
5. Lestor, *Coping* p. 58.
6. Sofield, *Design* p. 29.
7. Ibid, p.30.

Chapter 3
Anger Reconciliation: A Way to Harmony

1. Dr. Carter *The Anger Trap* p. 34.
2. Tim La Haye and Bob Phillips, *Anger Is a Choice* (Grand Rapids, Michigan, Zondervan Publishing House 1982) p.33.
3. Sofield, *Design* p. 132.
4. Dr. Henry Cloud and Dr. John Townsend, *Boundaries* (Grand Rapids, Michigan Zondervan Publishing House 1992) p. 35.
5. Lestor, *Coping* p. 43.

Chapter 4
Challenges to Using RAA

1. Dr. Carter, *The Anger Trap* p. 41

Chapter 5
Important Tools When Expressing Anger

1. Dr. Carter, *The Anger Workbook* p. 139.
2. Charles R. Swindoll, *Man to Man* (Grand Rapids, Michigan Zondervan Publishing House 1996) p. 127.
3. Dr. Carter *The Anger Workbook* p. 236.

Chapter 6
Conflict: A Path to Greater Intimacy

1. Carolyn Schrock-Shenk and Lawrence Ressler, *Making Peace with Conflict* (Scottdale, Pennsylvania Herald Press 1999) p. 26.
2. Dr. Carter, *The Anger Trap* p. 61
3. Ibid. p. 142
4. Sofield, *Design* p. 56.
5. Lestor, *Coping* p. 92.
6. Gary Oliver and Carrie Oliver, *Mad About Us* (Bloomington, Minnesota, Bethany House Publishers 2007) p. 143.
7. Joyce Hocker and William Wilmont, *Interpersonal Conflict* (Madison, Wis. William C. Brown Communication 1978) p. 32.

Chapter 7
Taking Responsibility for Our Anger

1. Edwin Lewis Cole, *Maximized Manhood* revised version (New Kensington, Pa. 2001) p. 104.
2. Sofield, *Design* p. 58.
3. Lestor, *Coping* p. 101.
4. Ibid. p. 102.
5. Dr. Carter, *The Anger Trap* p. 147.
6. Dr. Carter, *The Anger Workbook* p. 221.

To order copies of the book *Anger Reconciliation* ($13.95 each*),
or to schedule speaking engagements for James Offutt,
please e-mail James Offutt at offutt2@hotmail.com,
or order from www.angerispositive.com.
Your comments on the book are also welcomed.

Please include the appropriate sales tax if you are ordering from
New York State and include $2 for shipping.

10 % discounts for orders of 10 or more books